Ordinary Faithful People

Ordinary Faithful People

ROBERT L. HUBBARD, JR.

While this book is intended for the reader's personal enjoyment and profit, it is also designed for group study. A leader's guide with Reproducible Response Sheets is available from your local bookstore or from the publisher.

VICTOR BOOKS®

A DIVISION OF SCRIPTURE PRESS PUBLICATIONS INC.
USA CANADA ENGLAND

Permission to quote "Great Is Thy Faithfulness" is granted by Hope Publishing Company.

Permission to quote "Heart Touch" by Ruth Harms Calkin is granted by Tyndale House Publishers, Inc.

Material in chapters 1 and 12 originally appeared in the December 1987 issue of *Moody Monthly*.

Unless otherwise noted, Scripture quotations are from the *Holy Bible, New International Version,* © 1973, 1978, 1984, International Bible Society. Used by permission of Zondervan Bible Publishers; other quotations are from the *New American Standard Bible* (NASB), © the Lockman Foundation 1960, 1962, 1963, 1968, 1971, 1972, 1973, 1975, 1977; and the *Authorized (King James) Version* (KJV).

Copyediting: Carolyn Newhouse and Barbara Williams

Cover Design: Scott Rattray

Cover Photo: Jay Maisel Photography

Library of Congress Cataloging-in-Publication Data

Hubbard, Robert L., 1943–
    Ordinary, faithful people / by Robert L. Hubbard, Jr.
      p.   cm.
    Includes bibliographical references.
    ISBN 0-89693-894-8
    1. Bible. O.T. Ruth—Criticism, interpretation, etc. I. Title.
BS1315.2.H83   1992
    222'.3507—dc20   91-30877
                                          CIP

---

1 2 3 4 5 6 7 8 9 10 Printing/Year 96 95 94 93 92

Contents

To Evelyn and
in grateful memory
of Philip Iverson

Preface

Without doubt, the story of Ruth is one of the best-loved Bible stories. Readers delight in the simple love story of Ruth and Boaz. They admire Ruth's devotion to Naomi and her courage in dealing with Boaz. They love the clever way Naomi schemes to arrange Ruth's marriage. They enjoy tracing Naomi's rise from the rags of tragedy to the riches of triumph.

The Book of Ruth, however, is more than just a nice love story. It is the story of how God saved a family. It is also the story of how God gave David, one of the country's greatest leaders, to Israel. And it is about the kind of people God uses. The chapters which follow aim to open up its message for Christians today. My hope is that it will encourage you.

Special thanks are due to several people. As always, I express thanks for my family's love and support. They tolerated my preoccupation with writing this book. Special thanks also go to my faculty colleague, Dr. Dennis Williams, who put me in contact with Victor Books. I owe additional thanks to Mrs. Jeanette Freitag of Denver Seminary for editorial assistance.

Finally, I am grateful to many friends whose stories I used as illustrations. To avoid embarrassment, I have changed most of their names. Of course, they will know who they are!

It is very appropriate that I dedicate this book to my wife's parents, Mr. and Mrs. Philip Iverson. Truly, they are some of the "ordinary Christians" I am writing about. More personally, I want to honor their love, encouragement, and example over many years. I only hope heaven has a bookstore so Phil can see this book.

Chapter One

Introduction: God Wears Your Clothes

According to a recent story, two cows peacefully grazed in a grassy field one day. As they ate, a milk truck passed on the road beside the pasture. Its bright, attractive sign proudly announced: "Milk—Homogenized, Pasteurized, Vitamin-Enriched." Pondering that claim a moment, one cow said to the other, "Sorta makes a girl feel inadequate, doesn't it?"

Down deep we all feel inadequate about something. Whether at home or at work, we feel not quite up to some things. In one sense, the Bible enhances that feeling. How inferior we feel before its leading characters! Who of us compares to Abraham, the great man of faith? Armed with nothing but God's promises, he left his homeland in Mesopotamia for parts unknown. What about Moses, the founder of the nation of Israel? He was one of a kind—the only prophet "whom the Lord knew face to face" (Deut. 34:10).

And what about Paul? Tirelessly he traveled the Mediterranean world to spread the Gospel. Shipwrecks, beatings, angry crowds, sickness, and criticism hardly slowed his steady steps. And think of the many others: Deborah, Samson, David, Isaiah, John the Baptist, and Peter.

Famous Christians living today also make us feel spiritually inadequate. We admire Billy Graham and his many crusades around the world. We stand in awe of Mother Teresa and her work among the sickly poor of Calcutta. Closer to home, we look up to our pastor, the missionary who spoke at Wednesday prayer meeting, and the person who runs the rescue mission downtown.

The problem, however, is that these are all heroes. We see them as superhuman—a special breed of people different from ourselves. They are great people who achieve great things for God. They topple giants, rout armies, create empires, and work miracles.

By contrast, our lives seem so powerless and unimportant. Terrible giants and awful armies still freely roam our realm. But our little world looks more like a pitiful refugee camp than an empire. And our feeble hands have done no miracles.

This view of things also shapes our view of the kingdom of God. To us, it is like a professional football team owned by God and coached by Jesus. Each year, the owner and coach "draft" players for the team. They particularly prize "sharp" Christians—those who are outgoing, smart, and good-looking. (Theologians who know nothing about football call this a "call to the ministry.")

To prepare for the game, the coach puts them through rigorous training camps called Bible college or seminary. Only those who conquer such ordeals make the team and play the game. Only they can fill prestigious team positions like pastor, evangelist, and missionary. Only they are fit to take on the opposing team, Satan's famous players.

Where do we think ordinary Christians fit? We believe that our place is along the sidelines, not in the game. Our primary job is to keep the players on the field. So we issue paychecks, keep team records, and maintain equipment. During the game, we cheer the players, repair broken gear, and distribute water and towels.

In short, we belong to the team but are not really players. And here is what makes us feel even less important—we actually outnumber the players!

No wonder we battle discouragement and guilt. We feel like part-time Christians or second-class citizens in the kingdom. Our daily chores—raising a family, washing clothes, working at the factory, running office errands—do not seem

10

to count for much in God's eyes. Such mundane matters hardly sound like heroics of biblical proportions!

Finally, way down deep, we resent God's unfairness toward us. We do not feel "called" to full-time ministry, yet we think that is what God really wants. We long to know that our daily lives contribute something to God's work.

There is good news, however! God put the Book of Ruth in the Bible to encourage people like us. It gives a glimpse of God's work in such "ordinary" Israelites—in people like you and me. Indeed, as we shall see, it teaches a helpful truth: God uses the daily faithfulness of ordinary people to do great things. Further, through the story's main characters, it illustrates the specific traits of daily faithfulness.

Those traits are the subject of the chapters which follow. Each chapter will focus on a specific scene of the story. Each will study the trait of faithfulness which dominates that scene. All together, they paint a portrait of the kind of person which God uses—the kind of person we want to be. At the same time, the chapters will show how God relates to the story. They will teach us about how God relates to our lives today.

But before delving into God's teachings on faithfulness, we should cover some background on the Book of Ruth. We need to know about its author and why he wrote the book. We also need to learn what it teaches about God's guidance and His rewards for faithfulness. Then we will be ready to study the book scene-by-scene.

The Book's Background

Who wrote the Book of Ruth? The question is difficult to answer since the Bible does not tell us. One Jewish tradition gave the credit to Samuel, but that seems unlikely. Since the book ends with David (Ruth 4:17, 22), it was certainly written after he became king of Israel (about 1000 B.C.). By that time, Samuel was dead.

More likely, the author was someone on the palace staff in Jerusalem. The closing genealogy (vv. 18-22) suggests that the writer had access to royal records. Further, the story itself shows that he knew a lot about David's ancestors. It is likely that only someone with ties to the palace could get such information.

The story of Ruth also indicates that the author knew the stories of Abraham, Isaac, and Jacob. That might also point toward an author from the palace, as royal officials were often responsible for preserving knowledge of the kingdom. On the other hand, the writer may have been a descendant of David himself, though not necessarily royalty. Such a person would be familiar with the patriarchs as ancestors.

Whoever the author was, everyone agrees that the person was a great writer. He cleverly used wordplays and word repetitions to knit the story together. For example, he used the same Hebrew word (*kānāp*) to mean "[bird's] wings" in 2:12 and "garment edge" in 3:9. The pun makes a very important point. By marrying Ruth, Boaz gave her protection (i.e., covered her with his "garment edge"). And that protection was also the means through which Yahweh protected her (i.e., she found refuge under Yahweh's "wings").

Further, the author knew how to tell a story well! In chapter 2 he used a technique called a "flashback." When Ruth went to Boaz's field, the writer could have described her actions as they happened. Instead, after the fact, he reported them by quoting Boaz's foreman (2:7).

The author also knew how to keep the reader in the dark until just the right moment. For example, in chapter 3 he kept a crucial fact secret—that, besides Boaz, there was another relative who might marry Ruth. He let Boaz reveal that complication later (3:12)—at the very moment we think that he and Ruth are engaged! He also hid the fact that David descended from Ruth and Boaz until the very end (4:17).

When did this great author write the book? As noted earlier, he must have written after David had become king. Further, the book itself implies that the author wrote several centuries after the book's events. He knew that the judges ruled Israel a long time ago (1:1). Though we cannot be certain, it seems likely that the author wrote Ruth during the reign of Solomon (ca. 971–931 B.C.).

Introduction

What is the book's purpose? I think its primary purpose was to show that God had appointed David as Israel's king. It did this by telling how God Himself kept David's ancestors alive. Some people might think that David became king simply by beating his weaker rivals. The Book of Ruth, however, told about God's guidance of David's ancestors. That guidance implied that David was God's chosen leader for Israel.

This purpose suited the political situation during the reigns of David and Solomon. Their empire was truly a great one. We tend to think that all Israelites welcomed David's rule. The empire rested, however, on a shaky alliance between the two kings and Israel's two major power blocks.

One was "Judah," the southern block which first made David its king (2 Sam. 2:4, 11). The other was "Israel," the northern block of tribes which only later accepted his rule (5:3-5). In reality, personal loyalty to David and Solomon was the glue which held the nation together.

Two specific events illustrate how shaky the arrangement was. The first was the coup attempted by David's son, Absalom (2 Sam. 13–18). Apparently, the northern block was unhappy with David's rule. Absalom played on that discontent to seize power for a short time (15:1-6). The second event was the nation's quick division after Solomon's death (1 Kings 12).

Evidently, the northern group believed that some of Solomon's policies were too harsh. When Rehoboam succeeded Solomon, they asked him to relax them, but he refused. So the angry northerners refused to renew their commitment to the Davidic dynasty. Instead, they left Judah to Rehoboam and formed a country of their own which they called Israel. It would seem that the Book of Ruth was written to support the Davidic monarchy in the face of such underlying hostile feelings.

Finally, what kind of literature is the book? Literarily, it is a short story about the pious ancestors of King David. In biblical literature, a "short story" is a fairly short, self-contained narrative about earlier history, especially events involving ancestors. Other examples of biblical short stories

13

include the life of Joseph (Gen. 37–50) and the search for a wife for Isaac (Gen. 24). The purpose of the short story was to teach biblical lessons in an enjoyable way. Such an approach made them easy to remember.

God Wears Your Clothes

Two things about the Book of Ruth immediately catch our attention. Through these, the book teaches us about God's guidance of events. First, the book seems much closer to where we live than most of the Bible. We think, "Hey, this stuff sounds like my life!" There is good reason for that insight. The book's main characters are not heroes but ordinary people. There are no kings, generals, judges, prophets, or priests. Instead, the story is about an old widow, a young immigrant from Moab, and a leading businessman.

The story also takes place in a town like ours. It is not set in the capital, Jerusalem, near the corridors of political power. It is not set in a major city like Megiddo or Shechem. Rather, the events happen in Bethlehem, a town about six miles south of Jerusalem.

Bethlehem was an average town like many of our towns or suburbs. It sits just off the ancient "interstate" which ran between the capital and Hebron. It was probably little more than a pit stop for travelers—a place to eat and to spend the night.

Further, events take place in common places. The book has no stunning palace or gleaming temple. Instead, it features a farm field (Ruth 2), a public threshing floor (Ruth 3), and the local courthouse (Ruth 4). Further, the book is not about great matters of state or theology. It is about ordinary human problems—making a living, getting married, having children, and bearing grief. In sum, the book shows us life as we know it.

The second striking thing about the book is this: it seems to be rather secular in outlook. Granted, its characters frequently mention God (see 1:20-21; 2:4; 4:14; etc.). But He does not play a direct role in the story. In fact, God acts directly only two times in the whole book (1:6; 4:13). Instead, acts and choices by the human characters dominate. One almost has the impression that they are operating totally on their own.

Further, notice that the book has no miracles or grand displays of God's power like other biblical narratives. No rivers opened to let Naomi and Ruth cross from Moab to Judah on dry ground (cf. Josh. 3:15-17). No angel guided Ruth past fields owned by others to the one owned by Boaz. No burning bush briefed Naomi on how to arrange Ruth's marriage to Boaz. No dream or vision told Boaz how to obtain the legal right to marry Ruth.

In fact, there is evidence that the author actually wanted to downplay God's involvement in the story. At key points in the story, he could have commented on how God had guided things. Other biblical writers certainly did that (see Jud. 14:4; 2 Sam. 17:14). Instead, he simply described them as coincidences. For example, he says that Ruth just happened to choose to glean in Boaz's field (Ruth 2:3). And it just happened to be at about the time that Boaz himself visited there (v. 4).

Are we supposed to think that God is not involved? Of course not. But the author took this approach for a purpose. He wanted to teach us something important about how God works. For example, how do we respond when we read in Ruth that something "just happened"? Immediately we react, "Like fun it 'just happened'! God's behind it!"

That is exactly the reaction the author wanted. Cleverly, by playing down God's role, the author makes us all the more suspicious of His involvement. As one scholar said, in the Book of Ruth "chance" is just a kind of code for God's hidden activity.[1]

At the same time, the characters keep readers very aware of God's presence in the story. For example, they often give blessings and wishes for God's help. They create the impression that, as the human characters act, God is indeed at work—He is just offstage, behind the scenes. Look at the joyous exclamation of the women which opens the final scene (4:14). They praise God for giving Naomi a new baby.

That praise is especially significant. The women credit God with providing the baby even though, according to the story, God had directly done nothing except grant Ruth pregnancy (v. 13). Indeed, human actions guided everything else that led to the birth. It was Ruth who decided to migrate to Bethlehem and to go gleaning in a field there. It was Naomi who played the matchmaker and Ruth who agreed to carry out her plan. It was Boaz who convened the local elders to settle things legally.

How, then, can the women (and, through them, the author) give God the praise? The answer is simple: they (and the author) believe that God's providence actually guided what the characters did. Invisibly, from behind the scenes, God had acted. He is not one of the main characters, but in the end God turns out to be the story's true hero!

That is what the Book of Ruth teaches about God's involvement in the world. Sometimes, God intervenes directly to accomplish His purpose. The Bible is full of such occasions—the plagues in Egypt, Jesus' healing of lepers, God's raising of Jesus from the tomb.

Other times, God acts as He did in the Book of Ruth. He acts through the acts of His people—people like you and me. Our actions are really His actions. They are His cradling arms and supportive legs, His consoling voice and listening ear. At such times, God wears work clothes—ours!

Faithfulness Is Usefulness

Now, how does that work? How does God work through us? The Book of Ruth gives a simple answer: God works through our faithfulness. In Hebrew, faithfulness is *hesed,* a word which means "loyalty, kindness, compassion" (see Ruth 1:8; 2:20; 3:10). To be faithful is to act in a way that shows we are loyal to God. To be faithful is to treat other people with kindness and compassion. In short, to be faithful is to please God in what we do. Such faithfulness in daily tasks makes us useful for God's purposes. Faithfulness is usefulness.

But there is another aspect to remember. The Book of Ruth teaches that God rewards people for their faithfulness.

Introduction

Faithful deeds earn rewards from God. Two statements in the book mirror this truth. In 1:8 Naomi wished that God would show Ruth and Orpah the same "kindness" (*hesed*) they had shown her. Clearly, Naomi thought that God should reward their kindness.

Similarly, in 2:12 Boaz asked God to repay Ruth fully for her devotion to Naomi. Strikingly, the words Boaz used were money terms. In essence, Boaz said, "God, pay Ruth the full wages her work earned." Like Naomi, Boaz believed that God was inclined to honor such devotion. Hence, he wished that Ruth would receive her reward.

Is this what some call "works righteousness"? Not at all. The point is not that God *must* reward human good deeds. Both Naomi's and Boaz's statements are wishes, not commands. As such, they show that they understand God is sovereign. He can freely grant or deny their pleas. But they do appeal to the biblical teaching that, in His grace, God often rewards actions which please Him.

A biblical analogy might further illumine the point. We are all familiar with the biblical principle that as you sow, so shall you reap (Gal. 6:7). That is, human deeds are like seeds sown in the ground. When cultivated, they will in time produce results. And the quality and quantity of those results match the quality and quantity of the seeds sown.

For example, if one sows many evil deeds, evil results will soon sprout up. The greater the number, the greater the disasters which follow. Those who abuse family and friends will soon have neither. Those who unfairly mistreat employees will soon see their productivity fall. Those who abuse their own bodies will soon suffer symptoms of sickness.

By the same token, from good deeds spring good results. Those who care for family and friends will likely enjoy the love of both. Those who praise employees will soon see their productivity rise. Those who care for their own body will enjoy good health. In sum, the Book of Ruth encourages welldoing as the means to produce God-honoring results. To cultivate the traits of faithfulness which it describes is to sow seeds for God's glory.

The Book of Ruth illustrates this point well. The provision of an heir for Naomi sprouted from the loyalty of Ruth and Boaz. Ruth was the one who abandoned her homeland to accompany Naomi (Ruth 1:16-17; 2:11). Later, she bravely undertook two risky ventures. She gleaned in a public field to get food and made a midnight visit to Boaz to arrange a marriage.

For his part, Boaz treated Ruth kindly on the field. Generously he provided her with food, water, and protection (vv. 8-16). Willingly he played the role of kinsman-redeemer. He went to court to get the right to marry Ruth (4:1-8). Then he claimed her as his wife.

The story tells how God richly rewarded them. Happily, they became parents—a first for Ruth and perhaps for Boaz. Their child finally filled the bitter "emptiness" which had grieved Naomi (1:20-21; cf. 3:17). It supplied the heir to ensure her family's survival. That explains the joy which surrounded the book's closing scene, the meeting of Naomi and her newborn "son" (4:14-16).

More important, these faithful people turned out to be the ancestors of King David (v. 17). God used their faithfulness to give Israel a great new leader.

Conclusion

"Sorta makes a girl feel inadequate, doesn't it?" the cow said after reading the milk truck's claim. At times, the Bible makes us feel similarly inadequate. We wonder, "Does God use ordinary people?" The Book of Ruth answers with a resounding yes! It teaches that God uses the daily faithfulness of ordinary people to do great things for Him. Indeed, God sometimes wears our work clothes! That is, He acts through our deeds of faithfulness.

So, the Book of Ruth offers encouragement to ordinary people. It portrays those personal traits which please God, the ones which God rewards. We now turn to study those traits of faithfulness. The story of Naomi, Ruth, and Boaz will be our faithful guide.

Chapter Two

Perseverance: Faithfulness Endures Trial

Ruth 1:1-5

How suddenly and unexpectedly the tragedy struck. For two decades his amazing skills had dazzled countless crowds. Opponents feared facing his clever ball-handling and sure-shooting. Indeed, they sighed great relief when he retired from professional basketball in 1981. Six years later, after a friendly pickup game in a church gym, "Pistol Pete" Maravich collapsed and died of heart failure. He was forty-one years old.

Such tragedy is all too common. Every day the newspaper confirms that sad fact. No doubt, you could add your own examples. A loving husband and father, apparently in the best of health, suddenly falls sick and dies. "It was cancer," the coroner explains.

After a high school game, a bright, happy teenager ferries friends for pizza. "We'll give you a basketball scholarship," the college recruiter had said. Suddenly, the teen's car collides with one driven by a bleary-eyed drunk. "She's permanently paralyzed below the neck," the doctor says.

Widowed and penniless, a young woman slaves to raise three small children. Happily, she succeeds. But near retirement, her employer goes bankrupt. Scavenging creditors gobble up her only nest egg, the company retirement fund. "Sorry, ma'am, but it's within the law," the judge rules.

The Bible is well aware of life's tragedies. Consider the

infamous story of Job. One day he's a millionaire with a large, lovely family. The next day he's a pauper, alone with his wife, and deathly ill. With good reason, he complained, "Man born of woman is of few days and full of trouble" (Job 14:1). As one newspaper columnist put it, "Life is short—and then you die."

Similarly, the Book of Ruth opened with several tragedies. Our first task is to understand them. They provide the dark backdrop for the rest of the book. They will also teach us something about the first trait of faithfulness—perseverance.

A Sad Beginning

The Book of Ruth took place back when judges ruled Israel. The "era of the Judges" came between the death of Joshua and the coronation of King Saul (ca. 1200–1050 B.C.). Judges like Deborah, Gideon, and Samson were usually military heroes who saved their homeland from foreign invaders. Centuries later, Israel still remembered them as famous heroes (2 Kings 23:22; cf. 2 Sam. 7:11).

Those were very troubled days. According to the Book of Judges, it was a time when Israel turned to idolatry (Jud. 2:11-19). Again and again Israel left Yahweh to worship other gods. Only when Israel repented and cried for rescue did God raise up a judge to expel the invaders. Nevertheless, an apostate form of Israelite religion apparently took root in the north and attracted many Israelites (Jud. 17–18).

The Judges' era was also a time of civil war. At one point, eleven of the tribes of Israel almost killed off the tribe of Benjamin for a terrible crime (Jud. 19–21). They probably squabbled over other things too. So the time when Naomi, Ruth, and Boaz lived was an unstable, violent, and apostate one for Israel.

Sadly, the story of Ruth opened with two somber events (Ruth 1:1). First, a famine struck Israel. In Bible times, famines were common in the land of Canaan (Gen. 12:10; 41:54; 2 Kings 8:1). Droughts, plagues of locusts, and crop diseases were frequent causes (Deut. 28:42; 1 Kings 8:37; Joel 1:4; Amos 4:9). The second sad event resulted from the first. The food shortage forced a small family from Bethlehem—Elimelech, his wife Naomi, and their sons Mahlon and Kilion—to move to Moab, a country along the eastern shore of the Dead Sea.

The Bible tells us Elimelech's family went there "to sojourn." The Hebrew word "to sojourn" (*gûr*) meant "to live as a resident alien" in a foreign land. In the ancient East, the sojourner's legal status was like that of a person carrying a "green card" today. The best biblical example of this lifestyle was Abraham, who emigrated from Mesopotamia to live as a resident alien in Canaan, Egypt, and Philistia (Gen. 12:1-10; 21:34).

The life of sojourners was not a happy one. First, they were social outsiders. While modern society loves mobility—the freedom to live wherever one wants, even away from family—the ancient Semites valued sinking deep roots in one place. They prized strong family ties, ancestral property, and continuity with their past. Those were the very things the resident aliens lacked. So wherever they lived, they always remained outsiders. People tolerated them but did not want them.

Second, as foreigners, sojourners could be easily abused. At home, their extended family protected them from oppression and unfairness. In another land, however, they had no such protection. Even the highly honored Semitic custom of hospitality offered no help. Citizens of the host country could still take advantage of them.

During college days, I spent two summers as a minister among migrant workers. I can still see the dumpy camps they called "home." They were groups of simple shacks hidden in the corner of a farmyard. Laundry waved wildly in the wind. Their muddy streets became lakes in rainstorms. My knowledge of Spanish was the door into their world.

My "door," however, raised a wall between them and the outside world. If an owner cheated them of wages, they could do nothing about it. Poor pay made doctors' fees a luxury—unless the pain became unbearable. Sometimes, the sheriff might hustle a noisy drunk off to jail, but for the most part, he gave them little protection either from others or themselves. My migrant friends were outsiders—poor, foreign, vulnerable. So were Elimelech and his little family.

Worse, they lived in Moab, of all places! Moab was one of Israel's enemies. Over the years, Israel and Moab bickered like a pair of jealous brothers. In fact, Jacob and Esau probably got along better! Israel thought she had a good reason to look down on Moab. She was the proud descendant of Abraham. By contrast, Moab was born from Lot's seduction by his oldest daughter (Gen. 19:30-37). All this means that Ruth 1:1 would be like a modern writer starting a story with, "In 1946 a certain Jewish family went to Germany."

Despite the shame and danger, the migration was a necessity for Elimelech and his family. Moab had what Bethlehem lacked—food. So the little family settled there (Ruth 1:2).

More Tragedy

In *Paradise Lost,* poet John Milton wrote:

Me miserable! Which way shall I fly
Infinite wrath and infinite despair?
Which way I fly is hell; myself am hell;
And in the lowest deep a lower deep,
Still threat'ning to devour me, opens wide,
To which the hell I suffer seems a heaven (Book IV, lines 73–78).

Milton's words capture the agony of human "hell on earth." One barely bearable hell seems a heaven compared to the abyss below it! How often life seems like a prizefighter pounding us. Blow after blow beats us. Once settled in Moab, two bitter blows battered Elimelech's family.

First, Elimelech, Naomi's husband, died (Ruth 1:3). Strikingly, the author supplied no details about the circumstances. We wonder, "How long after his arrival did it happen? Did he die accidentally, of disease or old age, or foul play? Did God strike him down as punishment? Was God angry that he migrated to Moab in the first place or that he stayed too long?

Did God regard the move as disobedience or a lack of faith?"

But the death raised a more obvious question. In fact, a grieving woman hit me hard with the same question some years ago. The occasion was the funeral for her thirty-year-old brother, John, a fine, caring Christian man with leukemia. Like a brave soldier eluding hostile fire, he had moved in and out of remission for some months. Finally, the disease felled him. Tearfully, his heartbroken sister asked me, "Why did God let my brother die?"

Yes, that is the question—Why? Why did God let Elimelech die? The man's name meant "My God is King." Probably his pious parents gave it to him as an affirmation of their own faith. But the King apparently could not protect His loyal subjects! Or, might there be some purpose behind the tragedy? Might God salvage something good from it? As we shall see, the story's surprise ending will answer such questions.

For the moment, attention shifted to Elimelech's wife, Naomi. She was "left with her two sons." Suddenly, she was both a widow and a single parent—and in a foreign country too! Now, on her own, she must mourn her husband and raise her children.

In Moab, no caring kinfolk would join her grief and protect them from dishonest neighbors. To sojourn in Moab with a husband was one thing, to do so without him was quite another. One can almost imagine Naomi advising her sons with the words of a recent song, "It's you and me against the world!"

The Light That Failed

Unexpectedly, however, a small light flickered in the darkness. Each of Naomi's sons married a Moabite woman, one called Orpah, the other Ruth (Ruth 1:4). Ancient Israel welcomed marriage with the same joy that we do. For the families involved, it was a happy time of celebration and feasting. Such times reminded everyone of God's special gift of human love.

More important, marriage also gave the people hope for the future. Marriage opened up the possibility of children, and Israel believed that children were the key to life after death.

Though strange to us, Israel's concept of afterlife is very important background to the Book of Ruth.

Christians believe that to die is to go to be with Jesus Christ in heaven (2 Cor. 5:8). After physical death, life continues, but in a better, happier condition. By contrast, Israelites believed that they lived on in their descendants on earth. The life of their children kept them alive after death. In this case, dead Elimelech continued to exist in his two sons.

That is why Israel greeted the births of children with special joy. Children meant hope for life after death. That is also why Israel mourned childlessness so bitterly. One who died without children could not have life after death. For an Israelite, that was the most dreaded tragedy of all.

How did Naomi view the marriages? We do not know. Perhaps they soothed her grief somewhat. The marriages are important, however, for the progress of the story. They introduce the character Ruth, the person through whom the tale achieves its final conclusion.

And as the story progresses, we learn that they all lived in Moab "about ten years." This is not an unimportant detail. It hints that children might join the little family circle. Ten years is certainly enough time for at least one birth. Such happy additions would fan the story's flickering hope into a brighter flame. Children would shoo away at least some of the story's gloom.

Sadly, it was not to be. No children joined them. Instead, in Milton's words, "in the lowest deep a lower deep . . . opens wide." Naomi's present hell suddenly gave way to another, angrier abyss below. Both Naomi's sons, Mahlon and Kilion, also died in Moab (Ruth 1:5). Just how much more could one woman take!

Again, the nagging question, "Why?" confronts us. Were the deaths God's judgment? If so, for what—for marrying Moabites or for staying in Moab? The same questions plague all of us. In most cases, our only answer is a dark, uncertain silence. Here, the author offers only a similar, stern silence. He sounds like an accountant coolly totaling a ledger. He simply sums up the whole sad stay in Moab: "Naomi was

24

bereft of her two sons and her husband" (v. 5, NASB).

Four Hebrews left Bethlehem for Moab, only one remained. What a cruel joke that ancient enemy played on those poor souls! At first it offered the starving migrants life—food from Moab's rich fields. But behind that life lurked death. And how stealthily the monster pounced on its unsuspecting prey!

Now twin tragedies stared coldly at Naomi. First, she was a widow without family comfort and protection. If she were vulnerable to abuse before, how much more so now! She had to face a hostile world alone. Second, her family line now might cease to exist. There were no descendants. When Naomi died, Elimelech would have no one to keep the family alive. And Naomi's age made that event very probable.

So Naomi undoubtedly grieved. She and her daughters-in-law wailed bitterly over the graves of their husbands. The losses took their emotional toll on Naomi. One could write her epitaph in advance: "Died at 30. Buried at 60." On the outside, she looked like anyone else. Inside, she was dead—a walking corpse. Of her little migrant family, only she was left. And how long before the grave would snatch away even her?

Unless, of course, something were to avert that disaster. The reader wonders whether there was something that could be done. Did Israel have no means to save such a family line? If only Naomi could get back to Bethlehem! Would not her relatives offer help? Or would this truly be the end?

Two Reminders

The book's opening closed with many things unsettled. Painful unanswered questions trouble us. Why did this happen? Was God responsible? Was there a purpose in it? Let us be totally honest: such questions stick in our Christian craw! That discomfort, however, is just a symptom of something else.

Put bluntly, most of us are not used to unhappy endings, especially in the Bible. We expect Red Seas to part, attacking armies to flee, barren women to give birth, and corpses to come back to life. We remember that even the Bible's best known tragedy, the story of Job, had a happy ending.

As Christians, we want to live upbeat, optimistic, happy lives. And we want the Bible to help us. After all, we think that the Christian Gospel is good—not bad—news. If the Bible had an unhappy ending, we argue, unbelievers would not find the Gospel appealing. Who would surrender their lives to a God who could not be counted on to deliver in tough times?

Mass media preachers tend to confirm our inclination. Each week they proclaim a positive, optimistic outlook on life. One promotes "possibility thinking," another promises that "something good is going to happen to you." Even more radical, others proclaim that God wants us to be healthy and wealthy. They say that Jesus' atonement on the cross guarantees it.

All speak sincerely and with great conviction. None seem to profit personally from their views. And all back up their claims from the Bible. Again, let us be honest: down deep we hope they are right. The reason is that many heavy needs weigh us down. We earnestly yearn for some possibilities to conquer our impossibilities. We would like something good to offset the bad that afflicts our lives.

Now such theological optimism is not wrong. After all, the Bible is a very upbeat book. God is, indeed, fully able to heal awful diseases, lift sagging spirits, mend broken hearts, and save lost souls. Such optimism, however, fails two crucial tests. First, it conflicts with common human experience. The fact is that something bad has happened to many of us or to people we know. We personally know about almost unbearable suffering, suffering void of "possibilities" or good.

My faculty colleague, Dr. James Means, speaks of this in his book *A Tearful Celebration*. Reflecting on his wife's death from cancer in 1980, he notes how many Christians suffer experiences similar to his own:

> My experience is not unusual. I have been in hospital rooms with godly parents and heard their sincere prayers that the life of their child be spared. The child dies. Mis-

26

sionaries entrust themselves to God's safekeeping, but sometimes are murdered. Couples fervently ask God for a happy marriage, but presently they divorce. What happened to their prayers? Where is the Christian who does not have his own private tragedy to tell? (James E. Means, *A Tearful Celebration*, Portland, Ore.: Multnomah, 1985, p. 16)

Second, a one-sided Christian optimism overlooks God's priority for the Christian. In short, God is more concerned about our character than our comfort. He is more interested in our inner traits than in our outer trappings. The crucial evidence for this is the high value which the Bible places on suffering.

Recall what the Apostle James wrote: "Consider it pure joy, my brothers, whenever you face trials of many kinds, because you know that the testing of your faith develops perseverance" (James 1:2). To modern ears, James sounds like a sanctified masochist, "Hit me again, Lord, I love it!" But notice the item on God's agenda for us — perseverance. James teaches us to thank God for troubles because they toughen us for other hardships in life. They shape our character in ways that escape from them never could.

Consider also the case of the Prophet Hosea. God commissioned him to marry a prostitute (Hosea 1:2). Imagine bringing that bride home to meet your parents! But God knew what He was doing. By suffering his wife's unfaithfulness, Hosea learned something about God's relationship to Israel. He saw how unfaithful Israel had been to God. He saw how patient God had been with Israel. In the end, God's example taught Hosea patience, perseverance, and compassion. It showed him how to remain faithful to God despite a painful, shameful marriage.

The Apostle Paul graduated from the same school. When he asked to be healed, God said no. Instead, by living with pain, Paul learned to rely on God's strength rather than on his own (2 Cor. 12:8-10). God was more interested in Paul's inner strength than in his outer situation. Evidently Paul learned the lesson well. He reminded Christians at Rome, "We also rejoice in our sufferings, because we know that suffering produces perseverance; perseverance, character; and character, hope" (Rom. 5:3-4).

Like James, Paul celebrated suffering because it toughened believers with perseverance and character. He even believed that suffering increased our sense of hope. Behind suffering Paul saw the hand of the master Teacher, lovingly guiding His pupils through His curriculum for life.

Character Formation

Few jewels are treasured more than the simple pearl. Small wonder that imitation pearls stock store shelves everywhere. As someone has said, "Imitation is the highest form of flattery." So, those imitations pay high tribute to the supreme beauty of the genuine article.

Recall, however, how the pearl is formed. It results from an oyster's perseverance of an irritating grain of sand. Similarly, in God's plan, the irritating sands of trouble shape the beautiful pearl of endurance in our character.

This brings us to the first important reminder which Naomi's story gives: the Bible sees life with cold, hard realism. It pulls no punches, puffs no smoke screens, pitches no panaceas. Without apology, it tells the tragedy of Naomi straightforwardly as a fact of life. Precisely where, in God's plan, the story is headed still remains unknown. Only time—in this case, a very *short* time—will reveal its happy or unhappy ending.

Christians must face life under God with similar realism. Sometimes God mercifully spares us life's deeper, angrier abyss. Other times He may—for reasons known only to Him—let us plunge painfully into its angry depths. Amid our sorrow, we must simply follow the wisdom which Job stated amid his: "Naked I came from my mother's womb, and naked I will depart. The Lord gave and the Lord has taken away; May the name of the Lord be praised" (Job 1:21).

The second reminder of Naomi's story follows from this: God calls us to trust tenaciously in His goodness whatever

28

the circumstances. As Paul learned, that is the true test of faith. Awash in grief, it is difficult to affirm God's loving care. Battered by trial, one grudgingly sings God's praise. Psalms of lament more easily leave our lips! Yet, such is the life of faith—to cling to God when there is no reason to do so.

A simple poem sums up the matter well. It models the tenacious faith in suffering—the perseverance—which pleases God:

> A weathercock that once placed
>   A farmer's barn above,
> Bore on it by its owner's will
>   The sentence, "God is love."
>
> His neighbor passing questioned him,
>   He deemed the legend strange—
> "Now, dost thou think that, like the vane,
>   God's love can lightly change?"
>
> The farmer smiling shook his head.
>   "Nay, friend, 'tis meant to show
> That 'God is love' whichever way
>   The wind may chance to blow."
>   (Author unknown)

Chapter Three
Risk-Taking: Faithfulness Ventures Out
Ruth 1:6-13

In 1892, Julia Goniprow bid her native Lithuania farewell. Like so many others, she headed for America to start a new life. Later she poignantly explained the sorrow of parting, "The day I left home, my mother came with me to the railroad station. When we said good-bye, she said it was just like seeing me go into my casket. I never saw her again" (Mary J. Shapiro, *Gateway to Liberty* [New York: Vintage, 1986], p. 86).

That was the year America opened Ellis Island in New York harbor. Over more than three decades, 14 million immigrants passed through there. Behind them were tearful farewells on distant shores similar to Julia's. Departure for the "new world" meant leaving the "old world" behind. It meant saying "good-bye" forever to mothers and fathers, brothers and sisters, dear friends, and beloved places. Whatever the reason for leaving, the farewells were unbearably sad.

It is no wonder that immigrants called Ellis Island the "Isle of Tears." The tears were bittersweet. On the one hand, new arrivals cried for joy over a future life better than the one left behind. On the other hand, they wept for fear—fear of an uncertain future in a strange land. They wondered, "What lies ahead? Can I learn the language of America? Can I find work there? Will they mistreat me because I'm foreign? Will I fail? What will I do if I fail?"

That is the most dreaded word of all—failure. Nothing is

more devastating than to try something and fail. Watch the faces of losers in sports events. Some hide behind protective hands as if guilty of a great crime. Others stare coldly at the ground as if stunned by some invisible blow. Still others passively weep in silence like children ashamed of disappointing their parents.

The fear of failure haunts all our ventures. Students dread the ugly "F" on exams. "What if I can't make it in the job for which I'm studying?" they ask. On the job, employees fear the death sentence of failure, "Sorry, we don't need you around here anymore."

Parents anguish over how their children will turn out. Success or failure as parents hangs on whether kids can hold a good job, finish college, or choose the right mate. Married couples worry over weathering the stormy tides of life together. They fear the ultimate failure, a marriage cruelly shipwrecked on the rocks of divorce.

The fear of failure hung like dark, dreary clouds over the opening scene of the Book of Ruth (1:6-18). In it Naomi bid good-bye to her two daughters-in-law, Orpah and Ruth. They had started the journey to Judah together (vv. 6-7), but Naomi decided to return home alone. Twice her farewell kiss set off loud weeping among the women (vv. 9, 14).

Despite differences of race and age, deep bonds of affection apparently bound the trio. Through shared life and shared grief (vv. 4-5) they had become close. To end such closeness was plainly painful. For them, parting was anything but "sweet sorrow." Still, Naomi felt compelled to leave the younger pair behind.

Like the veterans of Ellis Island, fear of failure gnawed at them. Naomi wondered, "What does the future hold for me? What do I have to live for? As a widow returned from exile, will Bethlehem welcome me back with kindness? How will I support myself? Do my two friends know how risky it is for them to immigrate to Judah?"

No doubt, those friends pondered questions of their own. "Have we made the right decision to go with Naomi? Will they mistreat us in Bethlehem? Can we adjust to their customs? Should we go back to Moab?" As we continue, however, we see an unexpected, glorious light temporarily overshadow the scene's darkness.

As the next chapter will disclose, Ruth fends off Naomi's good-byes with a startling declaration of devotion. Her words teach us something important about faithfulness. In this chapter, however, we focus on Naomi's first attempts to persuade Ruth and Orpah to return to Moab. Her words teach us another dimension of faithfulness: the faithful Christian does what is right despite the risk of failure.

The Unseen Ally

The farewell took place somewhere down the road between Moab and Judah. Naomi's first words sound more like prayer than persuasion (Ruth 1:8-9). Probably, she expected the parting to be painful but short. But her companions resisted, making the conversation longer and more painful. Naomi had to work even harder to persuade the women to leave her.

Why did Naomi start the conversation after, not before, leaving Moab? The biblical author does not explain the matter. Ancient custom may underlie the procedure. It may have been customary for hosts to bid their guests farewell a ways down the road rather than at the front door. Certainly, these proceedings do seem to have a formality about them.

Whatever the background, the scene was a sorrowful one, particularly for Naomi. She stood to lose the most in the separation. For the younger women, the situation was actually the reverse of immigrants reaching Ellis Island. Back in their "old world," Moab, they could marry again and resume normal life. Naomi, however, faced no such happy future. Indeed, to lose the women was to lose her last links to her family.

On the other hand, the Bible took pains to explain why Naomi chose to return to Judah. Verse 6 says that "she heard . . . that the Lord had graciously looked after His people by giving them food" (see Robert L. Hubbard, Jr., *The Book of Ruth* [Grand Rapids: Eerdmans, 1988], 97). Over in Moab, Naomi heard good news from back home: God had given Judah food again! The famine which had sent her family into exile (v. 1) had come to an end. She could go home now. Perhaps she even viewed God's action as a sign that she *should* go back.

Three things in verse 6 bear a closer look. First, this was the first time that God acted directly in the story. In fact, He did not intervene again until near the story's end (see 4:13). As I noted earlier, the deeds of its main characters, not God, dominate the Book of Ruth. God's intervention here, therefore, signals His continued involvement in the story. Indeed, here His action caused Naomi to go home.

Second, God's action brought hope. Up to now, the book has told of nothing but a downward spiral of tragedies—famine, migration, death. By giving food, however, God started to reverse that tragic trend. Food ended the famine and Naomi's return ended the migration. Given that direction, we wonder whether death too might see reversal.

Third, the Hebrew verb "to look after graciously" (*pāqad*) gave God's intervention a particular meaning. Older translations rendered the word "to visit," but it means much more than to stay briefly. "To look after, take note of, to inspect" is more accurate. Often the verb describes how a superior "looks after" a subordinate (Gen. 40:4; Deut. 20:9; 1 Sam. 11:8). He does so to hold that subordinate accountable. The result of this "look" is either a reward or a reprimand.

Modern military people easily understand the idea. People from Washington often pay them a "visit." Surely it's no social call! Rather, a superior comes "to look after"—to inspect whether or not they are doing their jobs properly. If they are not, they get a good chewing out. If they are, they get a good word of praise.

The verb *pāqad* plays an important role in other Old Testament events. By using it here, the writer reminded readers of those other "visits" by God. God "looked after" barren Sarah and Hannah, and they conceived and gave birth (Gen. 21:1; 1 Sam. 2:21). He "looked after" Israel in Egypt—that is, He freed her from slavery as He promised (Gen. 50:24-25; Ex. 3:16; 4:31). Later, God promises to "look after" Israel by bringing her back from exile and providing her good leadership (Jer. 29:10; Zeph. 2:7; Zech. 10:3).

Thus, *pāqad* recalled two significant things. First, it stressed that God still cared for His people. Second, it implied that He might yet turn this story's tragedy into triumph. In sum, it said that God was still committed to doing good things for His people.

Here emerges the first lesson about risk-taking. God's care for us motivates us to take risks by serving others. We serve to express our gratitude to God for His great generosity toward us. Truly, "we love because He first loved us" (1 John 4:19). We take risks for God, not because we have to, but because we want to.

More important, God's care for us frees us to take risks without fear of failure. We know that He is with us every day to help us be faithful (Ex. 3:12; Matt. 28:20). We know that God's vast resources—wealth, power, an angelic army—are at our disposal (Rom. 8:32; cf. Gen. 22:15). As Elisha told his frightened servant, "Those who are with us are more than those who are with them" (2 Kings 6:16). We may be outmanned but never outgunned! His presence and help free us to take risks to help others.

I remember when God's commitment to me really hit home. In 1971, I was in Vietnam as a Navy chaplain. As a "circuit rider," I was always on the move visiting small bases in the Mekong Delta. I felt frustrated over the war and spiritually powerless to help my sailors and marines. Finally, at a place called Cho Moi, I hit bottom. A helpless feeling of despair overwhelmed me.

That afternoon, however, God gently spoke to me as I attended a Vietnamese village church. Since I spoke no Vietnamese, I prayed and meditated during the service. Suddenly, as if hearing someone sitting beside me, I heard Jesus' familiar words, "Upon this rock I will build My church, and the gates of hell shall not prevail against it" (Matt. 16:18, KJV).

What an encouragement! God's church rests securely on an unshakable rock, Jesus Christ. Jesus guaranteed that it would survive. Nothing—not even fiery hell itself—can defeat the church. Those great truths lifted my spirits. I did not need to fear failure. God reassured me of His commitment to me. With His power and presence, I could not fail!

God truly cares for us. He wants our lives to enjoy His blessing. He wants to enable us to live in a manner that honors Him. Nothing we do can improve on or take away from that. All He wants is our willingness to trust Him. He desires that we experience His help when we take risks to honor Him. He is ready for us to venture out into uncharted waters of faith.

The Tearful Talk

For the first time we hear the voice of Naomi. She began her farewell with a simple command: "Go back, each of you, to your mother's home" (Ruth 1:8). They were to head back to Moab by themselves and leave her to finish the journey to Judah alone. The ambiguous expression "mother's home" may refer to a mother's bedroom, the place where, according to ancient custom, marriages were apparently arranged. This implied Naomi's hope that the young pair might remarry.

Then she commended them into God's care with two wishes. First, she said, "May the Lord show kindness to you, as you have shown to your dead and to me" (v. 8). She meant more than just, "So long, and may God take care of you." In ancient Israel the phrase "may the Lord show kindness" was a formal way to terminate a relationship.

In essence, she said good-bye, handing them over to God's care. This was significant: entrusting them into God's hands showed how powerless she herself felt to help them. From Naomi's perspective, only God was able to care for them.

How was God to treat them? With the same kindness they had shown her. Here the book introduces the key word, "kindness." It is the Hebrew word, *ḥesed,* which points us to faithfulness as the book's main theme (see 2:20; 3:10). *Ḥesed* means "loving-kindness, loyalty, compassion" (see Micah 6:8). What "kindness" had Ruth and Orpah done? Naomi probably referred to their devotion to her since their husbands died.

The case of Tamar shows that young widows in Israel normally had two options (see Gen. 38). They could marry their husband's brother—the practice called levirate marriage (Gen. 38:8; cf. Deut. 25:5-10). Or they could live with their parents until another marriage was arranged (Gen. 38:11).

In this case, however, the first option was unavailable. There were no brothers for Orpah and Ruth to marry. The second option remained, but the women had not exercised it. They chose to live with Naomi rather than seek their own happiness in another marriage. They were even willing to follow her to Bethlehem.

Naomi's second wish (Ruth 1:9) amplified verse 8: "May the Lord grant that each of you will find rest in the home of another husband." The word "rest" meant more precisely a "place of settled security." Elsewhere it described the place where the ark found "rest"—that is, finally settled—after wandering among the Philistines (Ps. 132:8, 14). Biblical writers also applied it to Canaan as the Promised Land (Deut. 12:9; Ps. 95:11).

As widows, the young pair had suffered through an uncertain, anxious life. Naomi wished them a secure home with a loving husband. In her view, that was the proper reward for their loyal self-sacrifice.

Naomi's wishes teach us a second truth about taking risks. To take risks means to do what God, not the world around us, considers normal. It means to sacrifice our own desires and pursue what God wants. That may require us to deny ourselves what others have and to take up what others avoid. It leaves no room for "gusto-grabbing." Instead, it demands "gutsy-grabbing"—doing things the world might consider "abnormal" or even "strange."

Society prizes fame, but God calls us to humble service. Society loves people in the limelight, but God often places His people in hidden places. While society avoids unpleasant things, God honors those who quietly wash others' feet (see John 13).

In his popular book *Born Again*, Christian leader Charles Colson tells how he learned this lesson. Shortly after becoming a Christian, Colson faced a difficult decision. The Watergate scandal had forced him to leave his position as assistant to President Nixon. For months, his lawyers had sought to negotiate a plea bargain with the Watergate Special Prosecutor's office.

Colson would plead guilty to a misdemeanor and testify against other White House officials. In return, the prosecutors would agree not to indict him for a felony. For Colson, the difference between a misdemeanor and a felony was great. A misdemeanor would probably bring him only probation and he could continue to practice law. A felony conviction, however, meant a certain prison sentence and the loss of his license—and livelihood—as a lawyer.

There was only one problem: Colson was not guilty of the misdemeanor under discussion. The plea bargain required Colson to lie to save his own skin. Colson did much soul-searching. Finally, he decided that, as a Christian, he must not lie. His lawyer thought he was crazy, but Colson knew that he must tell the truth.

Thankfully, his fifteen-year-old daughter, Emily, confirmed his decision. One day, on the way home from the airport, he explained his situation. From the backseat, Emily asked bluntly, "Did you do what they want you to say you did?"

Colson answered, "No, I didn't."

"Well, then don't say you did it," shot back Emily.[2]

He didn't. He trusted God to care for his future and his family's welfare. He did what pleased his Lord rather than what pleased his lawyer. Colson was convicted of a felony and sent to prison. During imprisonment, God called him to the prison ministry which he now heads. Faithfulness to God demands a similar devotion of us. It asks us to do what is normal in God's eyes, not in the eyes of society.

Tough Talk

Naomi's sincere pleas failed to persuade her tearful companions. To the contrary, Ruth and Orpah insisted on going ahead with her to Bethlehem. The two sides stood at loggerheads along the roadside. To break the impasse, Naomi took a tougher approach. She again ordered them to "go back," then launched a blunt argument (Ruth 1:11-13). She argued that their devotion to her was too risky. To accompany her might bring them even greater tragedy.

She reminded them that they would lose any chance for remarriage. "I'm too old to have a husband," she said, "but even if I did marry, can I have sons?" The obvious answer was no. Naomi was no longer physically able to have children. She would never bear sons to marry Ruth and Orpah. If they wanted to remarry, they had better not stick with her.

But Naomi pushed the argument even farther. She appealed to the proverbial "bird-in-the-hand" principle. Suppose the impossible happened. Suppose she *did* bear sons. Why, she asked, should her young friends deprive themselves of marriage by waiting for them? In Moab, the odds were good that they could find husbands. Why pass up those good odds for the heavy odds against them in Judah? Why risk throwing away their future happiness?

To cap her argument, however, Naomi confronted Ruth and Orpah with another, even more frightening tragedy. She said, "The Lord's hand has gone out against me!" (v. 13) In the Old Testament, the phrase "the hand of the Lord" represented God's awesome power. It was His hand that defeated the mighty Philistines (1 Sam. 5:9). It was His hand that had given frightened Elijah courage (1 Kings 18:46) and eased Ezra's grief (Ezra 7:9, 28).

Naomi's remark was a startling revelation. Apparently, Naomi saw herself under attack by God and her lost family (Ruth 1:3, 5) as the carnage of that onslaught! For the women, the implication was obvious—and ominous. To accompany her was to risk sharing the next round of God's attack on Naomi. Why stay on the battlefield when there was opportunity for escape?

In sum, Naomi argued that the risks for Ruth and Orpah were too great in Bethlehem. Lifetime widowhood and tragedy awaited them. From Naomi's argument emerges a third truth about risk-taking: To take risks requires a willingness to accept the consequences.

Risk-Taking

To venture out for God means accepting the results with patience and determination. It means taking whatever comes as the price to be paid for the good to be gained. In this case, Orpah and Ruth would have to forfeit remarriage and risk more suffering. That was the price of devotion to Naomi.

It was late afternoon on December 1, 1955. At first, the bus ride home from downtown Montgomery, Alabama seemed routine. A dignified black woman headed home from her job as a tailor's assistant in a department store. Mrs. Rosa Parks occupied a seat in the "blacks-only" section. That was what the segregated bus system required. When the bus filled up, however, the driver asked her to surrender her seat to a white person.

Challenging the bus driver meant Parks might face dangerous consequences. He could expel her from the bus. She would then have to walk the great distance home. She could also be arrested, fined, and jailed. Confined, white jailers could abuse her without penalty. But Rosa Parks had had enough of such degrading indignities against blacks. She refused to surrender her seat. And the police arrested her for violating Montgomery's bus ordinance.

Mrs. Parks' arrest proved historic. It sparked the famous black boycott of the oppressive Montgomery bus system. That, in turn, furthered the civil rights movement of the '50s and '60s. That movement revolutionized racial relations in America. An ordinary Christian, Rosa Parks was committed to racial justice. She lived out her faithfulness by risking her personal safety on a bus. Willingly she accepted the consequences of doing what pleased God. Whatever the results, she determined to do God's will.

Conclusion

Those who follow Jesus Christ must take similar risks. Our witness for Christ on the job may bring criticism and misunderstanding. Still, we must witness. Our stand for morality may mean being labeled a "Puritan." Still, we must stand up for morality. To promote racial and economic justice, we risk being called "do-gooders." Still, we must promote justice.

The reason is that faithfulness requires risk-taking. It demands that we break with what the world calls normal and follow God's standard of normalcy. It asks that we willingly accept the consequences of our faithfulness.

At the same time, we must remember that we are not alone. God stands behind all our efforts. He cares that we succeed. He offers us His resources. Most important, He measures us by a different standard of success. Indeed, success in the world's eyes may be failure in His.

For the Christian, to succeed is simply to be faithful, to fail is to be unfaithful. As we venture out in faith, taking the risks necessary, our only aim is to do what pleases God. What risks might God want you to take?

Chapter Four

Commitment: Faithfulness Serves Others

Ruth 1:14-18

At first glance, Louella struck me as a typical, eccentric spinster in her early fifties. She had graying hair, plain clothes, drab makeup, and gold wire-rimmed glasses. Whenever she talked, her eyelids fluttered nervously, likely due to shyness. I marveled at her shiny twenty-year-old car. It had only 25,000 miles on it, and she chuckled at how much trouble the dealer had getting parts for it!

I soon saw another side to Louella, however. She attended the Navy chapel where I ministered as chaplain. Her late father had retired from the Navy, and her brother had been killed in World War II. One Sunday, she asked if I would visit her elderly mother at their home. She explained that the woman was ninety-two years old, bedfast, but still very alert. I made an appointment to do so.

On that visit, I learned the full story. Louella had never married. Instead, for nearly thirty years she had chosen to care for her widowed mother. The two of them lived simply on her mother's modest Navy pension. Louella had devoted her life to serving her elderly widowed mother.

That kind of commitment seems very old-fashioned these days. It recalls museum mannequins wearing clothes from 1890—fluffy lace blouses, bustles, Prince Albert coats, and top hats. Once the "in" fashion, such styles strike modern eyes as rather quaint. They are cute to look at, but who would want to wear them today!

The same is true of devotion like Louella's. Today's designer labels begin with the word "self"—"self-awareness" and "self-fulfillment." By contrast, the idea of commitment to someone else seems as quaint as 1890s clothes, as out of style as high-buttoned shoes.

The results of a recent major study confirm that truth regarding commitment. Over a five-year period, scholars interviewed 200 people across America. They wanted to know how people thought their private lives related to their public life as citizens. In the end, the researchers concluded:

> What has failed at every level—from the society of nations to the national society to the local community to the family—is integration: we have failed to remember "our community as members of the same body," as John Winthrop put it. We have committed what to the republican founders of our nation was the cardinal sin: we have put our own good, as individuals, as groups, as a nation, ahead of the common good (Robert N. Bellah et al., *Habits of the Heart*, New York: Harper & Row, 1985, p. 285).

Indeed, the words "me" and "now" guide the way many people live today. The "me" attitude says, *"I* am the center of my world. *My* dreams and wants are most important. I do what pleases *me."* People are so preoccupied with themselves that they forget about others. And society reflects it. More college students major in business and finance than in nursing or social work.

People prefer to live in nice, safe suburbs. If they can afford it, why put up with the noisy streets, ethnic minorities, and social riffraff of cities? Who cares that such moves rob millions of people of leadership, financial capital, and personal pride? A recent TV commercial sums up the suburban creed: "Go ahead, you've earned it." People think they deserve what they want. A spirit of selfishness grips the land.

And people want things now, not later. Alas, the idea of deferring anything to a future time is as foreign as creatures from Mars. Again, television sounds the slogan: "You only go around once in life, so you've got to grab for all the gusto you can." In short, everything must be done now.

Of course, there is some wisdom in that. Life is, indeed, short. And sometimes one must "strike while the iron's hot." Some things are best done now, for opportunity may not knock twice. Further, there is nothing inherently wrong with wanting to live pleasantly. There is no virtue in choosing crime-ridden neighborhoods over crime-free ones. The world needs both good business people and good health care people.

The problem is that God's agenda for His people is different from the world's. He honors self-denial, not self-indulgence. Self-sacrifice ranks much higher on His list than self-fulfillment. Whatever their vocation, God wants His people committed to others, not just themselves.

And that brings us to the focus of this chapter—commitment. The last chapter taught us that faithfulness requires us to take risks despite the threat of failure. We learned that lesson from Naomi's argument. In this chapter we will learn that faithfulness demands total commitment. This time we hear the voice of the Moabitess Ruth.

The Last Holdout

Naomi's roadside argument finally succeeded. In baseball terms, she batted a respectable .500. One of the women, Orpah, decided to return to Moab. This brought a moment of tense, teary drama. Weeping loudly, Orpah kissed Naomi good-bye, turned around, and headed eastward (Ruth 1:14). One can imagine the sorrowful form of Orpah slowly fading in the distance.

Now, of the three women who left Moab, only two remained. Indeed, Ruth not only remained, she clung tightly to Naomi. For a moment, grief overwhelmed the pair and all talk ceased. Their embrace was so tight that a passerby might have mistaken them for a single person. In the silence, however, the reader senses a turning point in the story. Something weighty, something crucial hangs in the balance—Ruth's final decision.

43

Literarily, the author fueled that suspicion in two ways. First, the Hebrew sentence structure of verse 14 painted a sharp contrast between Orpah and Ruth. It said, "Orpah kissed her mother-in-law good-bye, *but* Ruth clung to her" (italics mine), implying that the lives of the two Moabites might be headed in opposite directions. It hinted that Ruth probably would not follow in Orpah's footsteps. For the moment her resistance to Naomi's assault remained strong. But how long could her resolve hold out?

Second, the Hebrew expression *dābaq b^e,* meaning "to cling to, to stay close to," suggested that Ruth intended to join Naomi permanently. The phrase often described how someone willingly left one group to join another. For example, it is used of those who intermarry with non-Israelites, thus compromising their ties to God's covenant people, Israel (Josh. 23:12; 1 Kings 11:2).

Genesis 2:24, however, provides the best known example of its use: "For this reason a man will leave his father and mother and be united to [*dābaq b^e*] his wife, and they will become one flesh." The phrase conveyed the idea of firm loyalty and deep affection. A husband left his parents to form a family unit with his wife. Similarly, for Ruth to "be united with" Naomi meant to leave Moab behind (Ruth 1:16).

In sum, the Hebrew wording implied Ruth's commitment to join Naomi's personal circle permanently. In a stunning statement, Ruth will soon make that implicit commitment explicit.

Permit me a word of caution about Orpah, however. One can easily find fault with her choice. Indeed, many writers criticize her for taking the easy way out. But notice that the Bible fails to evaluate her decision. The silence might imply sympathy with, if not approval of, her actions. Further, remember that Orpah simply did what Naomi ordered. One might even praise her for her obedience. After all, she followed the wisdom of an elder person as Semitic culture taught.

Finally, observe her role in the story. Orpah represented ordinary, normal commitment. As a contrast, her choice set off Ruth's devotion as extraordinary. It underscored that, while Orpah's action was acceptable, Ruth's was exemplary.

One Last Try

Orpah may have inspired Naomi to make one last run at Ruth's resolve. Blunt argument had failed, so this time she tried a softer, subtler approach. Perhaps pointing down the road toward Orpah, Naomi said, "Look ... your sister-in-law is going back to her people and her gods. Go back with her" (Ruth 1:15).

Plainly, she applied old-fashioned peer pressure. Granted, Naomi had Ruth's best interests at heart. She truly wanted Ruth to be happy. Yet, she said in essence, "Don't be a fool, Ruth. Follow Orpah's good sense." The point was to make Ruth feel foolish for staying behind. It appealed to common human pride as being sensible. Ruth was to think, "Yeah, what a laughingstock I'd be in Judah — and Orpah happily married and raising her kids back in Moab!"

The appeal to peer pressure is a powerful argument. One of our deepest human needs is to be accepted by others. That need drives much of our behavior. In every society, a fool is the butt of jokes, the source of merriment for others. Who wants to look foolish in front of friends?

I see this force at work every time I take my two teenage sons shopping for clothes. Granted, they use different words for it, but it is the same thing. I point out what I think is a nice-looking shirt. But they reply, "No way, Dad. That's just not cool." In this context, the words "not cool" do not mean "chilly" or "cold," they mean "unacceptable to my peers." In other words, "If I wear *that*, Dad, I'll look stupid to my friends."

Now let me confess something. I recently felt the same pressure myself. After fifteen years, the exhaust pipe on my old car finally rusted through. The engine muffler could no longer muffle. Whenever I started the car, it belched a long, raucous *vroooom!* At first, I got a big kick out of gunning the engine, especially around my seminary students. Nothing like a crazy professor playing hot-rodder to get a few laughs!

The sound also brought back memories of my high school years. It reminded me of the '52 Plymouth with twin tailpipes which a friend owned. What a great *vroooom* echoed behind us whenever we revved up those six cylinders!

Gradually, however, enjoyment gave way to embarrassment. I thought of my poor neighbors enduring the roar of my "hot rod" starting up each morning. I wondered what they thought about this middle-aged professor reliving teenage memories.

Suddenly, my noisy car ceased to be "cool." While driving, I found myself avoiding people I knew. I feared they might hear that awful, raspy *vroooom*. I felt a little foolish. That embarrassment finally drove me to get the pipe fixed.

Naomi's appeal to Ruth was similar: "For goodness sake, Ruth, don't embarrass yourself. Don't be a fool!" Orpah had set a good, sane example. Ruth should follow it. That was only logical. So, our eyes now focused on Ruth. What thoughts lay behind her tears? Would she do what was sensible in human eyes? Or would she obey the dictates of a different logic—a logic even more compelling than Naomi's? Which way would Ruth go?

The Ultimate Rebuttal

Finally, Ruth had her say. And what a say it was! With rhythm and balance, the statement almost had the ring of poetry. It is one of the most memorable declarations in the entire Bible. In content, it conveyed a powerful sense of devotion. In the story, Ruth's words marked the scene's climax. They emphatically slammed the door on any return to Moab. They pushed the story irresistibly forward toward Bethlehem.

First, Ruth bluntly rejected Naomi's plea. "Don't urge me to leave you or to turn back from you," she said. Elsewhere, the Hebrew verb rendered "urge" meant "to fall upon, to attack" in a violent, physical sense (see Ex. 5:3; Jud. 5:12). The meaning here, however, is probably different. Naomi was not scratching and slugging Ruth as they talked by the roadside!

46

Instead, "urge" probably meant "to put pressure on." Ruth told Naomi, "Back off, will you! Don't lean on me anymore!" The pointed rebuff probably served two purposes. It answered Naomi with a loud, firm, final no! It also sought to stop Naomi from assaulting Ruth's determination again.

Second, Ruth published her own plans. To begin, she threw Naomi's plea back at her. Rather than "go back" to Moab, Ruth promised to "go with" Naomi wherever she went. She said, "Where you go I will go, and where you stay I will stay" (Ruth 1:16). Wherever the future took Naomi—on the road, in exile, or in Israel—Ruth would remain at her side. In sum, Ruth wrote Naomi a blank check of devotion. In the space labeled amount, she wrote "Wherever."

Further, Ruth adopted Naomi's nationality and religion. She said, "Your people will be my people and your God my God." Again, Ruth replied directly to Naomi's own words admonishing her to follow the example of Orpah who returned to "her people and her god" (v. 15). Ruth renounced her Moabite roots, both ethnic and religious. She embraced the nation and religion of Israel. From here on, Naomi's family would be Ruth's family and Israel's God, Ruth's God.

Today, we enjoy great social mobility and freedom of choice. For us to move from one place to another is no big deal. To mix with people of other races or to change one's religion is also no problem. My own heritage is a case in point.

On my father's side, my English ancestors immigrated to New England in the 1630s. On my mother's side, I descend from Swedish immigrants who settled on Nebraska farms in the mid-1800s. My paternal ancestors left New England to farm in Iowa just before the Civil War, then moved to California about 1910. My maternal grandparents moved to California about the same time.

As for religion, my English ancestors apparently were not religious. But, as a young person, my grandfather was saved in a Methodist revival in Iowa. He passed on Christianity to his children and grandchildren. Later Grandpa became a Pentecostal, but my father chose to be a Baptist. Meanwhile, my mother grew up in the old Swedish Covenant Church.

Now the point is that we regard such movements and changes as very normal. Because of American history, Americans view migrations as a matter of national pride. They also pride themselves on their religious tolerance. They accept religious migrations from one faith to another simply as an expression of personal freedom.

But our modern view of mobility gets in the way here. It dulls our ears to the full force of Ruth's words. By contrast, Ruth's statement would strike ancient readers as startling. Mobility had no part in Semitic culture. Semites saw themselves as inextricably bound both to their family and to its ancestral property. A clay tablet from Nuzi, an ancient city in northwestern Mesopotamia, illustrates this point. It tells how one father totally disinherited two of his sons for moving to another town.

In the Old Testament, the only comparable declarations are those of Rahab and Naaman (Josh. 2:11; 2 Kings 5:15). But Ruth outdid them both. Rahab and Naaman both confessed Yahweh as their God but remained with their families in their homelands (Josh. 6:25; 2 Kings 5:17-19). Ruth accepted Israel's God as her own, the nation of Israel as her new family, and the land of Israel as her new home.

Christian commitment is no different. It demands that we devote ourselves wholeheartedly to Jesus Christ and to His people, the church. We cannot straddle the fence on the matter. There can be no compromise. We must cut all ties to our past—to other gods and, if necessary, to our family. Recall Jesus' clear teaching on the subject. "No one can serve two masters. Either he will hate the one and love the other, or he will be devoted to the one and despise the other. You cannot serve both God and money" (Matt. 6:24; also Luke 16:13).

The analogy is clear. We may work for all kinds of employers. We may even work for one and moonlight for another. But it is impossible to work for both employers at the same time. No one can meet the demands of both simultaneously because both require our full attention.

By the same token, there are two competing spiritual em-

48

ployers, God and money. Both want to hire workers. No Christian can work for both. Both demand full devotion. A choice must be made.

What about family ties? Jesus taught that family loyalties cannot be more important than commitment to Him. He said: "Anyone who loves his father or mother more than Me is not worthy of Me; anyone who loves his son or daughter more than Me is not worthy of Me" (Matt. 10:37). Jesus did not mean that family loyalty is unimportant. He did not mean that love of family does not concern God.

No, the key word in Jesus' statement is "more." Jesus stressed that we must love Him *more* than family. The issue is: who has priority in our devotion? No other loyalty—family, friends, jobs, leisure interests—must stand between us and Jesus. Ruth showed that kind of commitment. She surrendered her Moabite family and faith for Israelite ones. So must we.

Ultimate Devotion

Ruth also went a decisive step further. Theoretically, she could have had her cake and eaten it too. Because of her age, Naomi would probably die within a few years. Ruth could have stayed with Naomi until her death and then returned to Moab. Even so she still might be young enough to remarry and bear children. That way she could serve Naomi and still live her own life later.

Carefully notice Ruth's words, however: "Where you die I will die, and there I will be buried" (Ruth 1:17). Ruth probably had Semitic burial customs in mind here. Normally, Semites buried all dead family members in a common grave. That is why, though in Egypt, Jacob insisted on burial with his parents and grandparents in the family plot near Hebron (Gen. 49:29-32; 50:13). The biblical phrase "to be gathered to [one's] people" probably alludes to this custom (25:8; 35:29; Jud. 2:10).

Ruth promised that she would die in Israel and be buried there with Naomi's family, effectively shutting the door on any future return to Moab. No one would carry her bones home like Israel did Jacob's! Israel was now her home and would be so after death. Naomi's family was now her family and would be so after death. As if to underscore her words, she swore an oath in the name of her new God, Yahweh.

Here Ruth models another aspect of commitment. True commitment is total and final. Unlike modern contracts, it allows no footnotes, no fine print, no exceptions, no conditions, no escape clauses. Once decided, there can be no turning back—or looking back.

Remember poor Lot's wife—a classic example of half-hearted commitment (Gen. 19:26). Even while fleeing doomed Sodom, she longingly looked back to her past life there. For a wavering will, God turned her into a pillar of salt!

True commitment, by contrast, requires steady steps forward. It demands eyes focused straight ahead. As Jesus said, "No one who puts his hand to the plow and looks back is fit for service in the kingdom of God" (Luke 9:62). Anything less is not the genuine article.

What about when death strikes the family? Do burial duties ever come first? Again, the answer was no. When a man asked for leave to bury his father, Jesus taught: "Follow Me, and let the dead bury their own dead" (Matt. 8:22). Jesus requires the complete devotion of all that we are and of all that we have. A contemporary chorus sums it up well:

I have decided to follow Jesus,
No turning back, no turning back.

Apparently, Ruth convinced Naomi that her commitment was unshakable. Naomi abandoned her persuasion tactics (Ruth 1:18). She saw that Ruth was "determined to go with her." *Determined* here meant literally "strengthening herself" (Heb. *'āmēts*, reflexive form). In other words, Ruth had mustered all her physical and spiritual powers to carry out her decision. Her eyes stared ahead toward Judah. No rebuttal could dent such determination.

For the first time, silence fell over the scene. Neither words nor wailing passed between the pair. Nothing more needed to be said. Verse 18 says that Naomi "stopped urging her."

Silence verifies the power of such commitment. Halfhearted commitment rightly stirs up talk. It deserves words like "hypocrisy" and "cowardice." It merits stern criticism. But silence greets total commitment—no objections, no rebuttals, no snide labels. It rings so true, so right, so free of dispute that one stands in awe of it.

That was true of Ruth's commitment, and it will be true of ours too. As the Apostle Peter wrote, "It is God's will that by doing good you should silence the ignorant talk of foolish men" (1 Peter 2:15). True commitment immediately proves that it is genuine. No one can object to it. That is what our commitment should be like.

Last Letter

Several years ago, I heard from my friend Louella again. Ten years had passed since my visits with her ninety-two-year-old mother. She wrote of her mother's death and of the memorial window which she gave the chapel to honor her parents and brother. Suddenly, from the distance of time and place, I saw how unusual Louella was.

At first glance, she seemed like an odd, eccentric woman—a kind of human antique that belonged in a museum. She had devoted her adult life to care for her feeble mother. But was she really eccentric? By modern standards, yes. But by biblical standards, no. Her eccentricity was in reality remarkable commitment. She was a modern Ruth.

The world could use more people like Ruth. If you are willing to be one of them, I suggest you pray the prayer below. Make it for you what Ruth's declaration was for her.

"Heart Touch"

Whatever our hands touch—
We leave fingerprints!
On walls, on furniture
On doorknobs, dishes, books.

Ordinary Faithful People

There's no escape.
As we touch we leave our identity.
O God, wherever I go today
Help me to leave "heartprints"
Heartprints of compassion
     of understanding and love,
Heartprints of kindness and
      genuine concern.

May my heart touch a lonely neighbor
Or a runaway daughter
Or an anxious mother
Or perhaps an aged grandfather.

"Lord, send me out today to
     leave heartprints.
And if someone should say,
  'I felt your touch,'
May that one sense Your love
Touching through me."*

*From: *Lord, Could You Hurry a Little*
By: Ruth Harms Calkin © 1983
Used by permission of Tyndale House Publishers, Inc.
All Rights Reserved.

Chapter Five
Transparency: Faithfulness Shows Feelings
Ruth 1:19-22

I buried a young man some time ago. The funeral was one of the most painful I have ever done. At age 27, this young man had taken his own life. Worse yet, the suicide took his family and friends by surprise. Before that fateful moment, he seemed to be doing well. He was married, had a good job, and seemed to enjoy many friends. Everyone thought that his life was pretty well "together." But inside something was desperately wrong.

Newspapers regularly report similar surprises. A young family man, well-liked by neighbors, suddenly guns down innocent people in a shopping mall. A famous athlete, long-admired for work with children's charities, is arrested for child abuse. A popular politician, about to win easy reelection, mysteriously disappears. A highly respected minister shocks his congregation by confessing marital infidelity. A common thread binds these cases: the person others knew was different from the person inside.

The poet Henry David Thoreau put his finger on the problem. He said: "Like cuttlefish we conceal ourselves, we darken the atmosphere in which we move; we are not transparent" (Bradford Torrey, ed., *The Writings of Henry David Thoreau: Journal Vol. 4* [Boston/New York: Houghton Mifflin, 1906], 315 [August 24, 1852]). Thoreau compares us to a common marine animal, the cuttlefish. The cuttlefish lacks the defenses of other fish—speed, size, shells, or poisonous spines. To protect itself, it pours out a dark, inky liquid as it moves. It safely hides from predators behind that murky camouflage.

Sadly, we all tend to hide ourselves from other people. In Thoreau's words, "we are not transparent." We are more a door than a window. The person we are inside is shut behind the door of the person we are outside. We shut people out so they cannot see who we really are. Like the cuttlefish, we surround ourselves with camouflage, keeping our inner emotions—outrage, grief, or joy—safely out of view.

I have observed several such camouflages. Some of us hide behind a "stone face." Such people seem to have the feelings of a stone wall. They maintain the same appearance at all times, in joy or sorrow. Indeed, were it not for an occasional eyelid blink, no one would know they were alive! Inside, stormy seas of emotion may be churning; outside, everything seems calm.

Others deploy the "happy face." Whatever the circumstances, these people always wear a cheery smile. This camouflage works like the football player's fake. It creates the impression of constant happiness when the opposite might be true. The deceptive smile cleverly masks the crying going on inside.

Finally, some Christians use what I call the "hallelujah face." These people welcome every situation—happy or sad, tragic or triumphant—with a hearty "Praise the Lord!" What makes this camouflage so effective is its spiritual sound. The person appears to be obeying the scriptural command, "In every thing give thanks" (1 Thes. 5:18, KJV).

Now it is hard to question such biblical fidelity! Sometimes the thanks is genuine. And some people are just happier by nature. Other times, however, the "hallelujah face" is just a bluff—a fake to cover up turbulent emotions or confusion inside.

However well-intentioned, such fakery charges a terrible price. First, the effort to maintain the front is exhausting—it takes work to keep the face in place! The hotter our inner emotions boil, the greater the effort required. And that effort robs us of energy which might be devoted to healthy endeavors.

Further, our body may betray the hidden inner turmoil. According to doctors, skin rashes, headaches, arthritis, and ulcers may be symptoms of emotional stress not properly expressed. How ironic! The body puts on display the very conflicts we desperately try to hide! Finally, hiding is a terribly lonely venture. It imprisons us in a very personal kind of solitary confinement. It walls us off from what we really need—deep, supportive, open friendship.

It is here that Naomi will teach us a lesson. In the closing scene of chapter 1 she modeled a transparent relationship with God. The lesson is a surprising one: transparency before God is an expression of faithfulness. It trusts that God understands our ugliest feelings. It assumes that God knows us just as we are—and accepts us anyway.

The Homecoming

Ruth's stunning statement had ended her roadside talk with Naomi. So the pair resumed the trip toward Judah. Indeed, the Bible writer hurried things along by omitting details of the trip. Ruth 1:19 simply reported that "the two women went on until they came to Bethlehem." The author was more interested in the arrival than the trip (vv. 19-21).

Certainly, we share that interest in homecomings. During my lifetime, I have witnessed two important, emotional homecomings on television. In 1974, I witnessed "Operation Homecoming," the return of American prisoners from North Vietnam. Through teary eyes, I saw the men held captive so long descend to freedom from an Air Force plane. Millions of fellow citizens celebrated their return.

Six years later, I witnessed the arrival of the American hostages released by Iran. This time, thousands of yellow ribbons tied to trees waved a cheery welcome. Again, my eyes teared. Both occasions were joyous. For the returnees, they meant freedom and reunion with families. For Americans, each signaled the end of a political standoff.

Naomi's arrival in Bethlehem, however, was different. The returns I witnessed were announced publicly in advance. By contrast, Naomi's return took Bethlehem completely by surprise. No one expected to see her in Bethlehem that day. That explains the town's reaction to Naomi and Ruth: "the whole town was stirred because of them" (v. 19).

The Hebrew word for "stirred" (*wattēhōm*) paints a graphic picture of this scene. The word meant "to resound, echo." In 1 Kings 1:45, it described how Jerusalem "resounded" excitedly when Solomon was crowned king. Similarly, 1 Samuel 4:5 reports how Israel's joyous shouts "echoed" when the ark of the covenant arrived in camp.

Bethlehem "was stirred." Happy townspeople hurried down streets shouting the news about Naomi. Soon the whole town hummed with excitement.

A group of women put the town's reaction into words. "Can this really be Naomi?" they asked (Ruth 1:19). The question was not really a question at all. The women were not asking to see Naomi's I.D. card! Rather, they were expressing their surprise at seeing her.

Their response was understandable. Naomi had been away for more than ten years (v. 4). Probably the town had heard little or nothing about her during her absence. Bethlehem had given her up for dead. Now the "corpse" had come back to life.

Though joyful, the women could hardly believe their eyes! They were probably unprepared for the angry outburst which their welcome set off.

The Outburst

Imagine what crosscurrents of feelings churned within Naomi that day. One current was a flood of joy. She was home—finally. How pleasant to enter Bethlehem's gates, to walk her narrow streets, to hug dear friends. The familiar sights, sounds, and smells brought back so many memories—childhood games in back alleys, the sweet smell of harvest fields, growth from girl to woman, marriage to Elimelech, the births of two sons.

Against that joyous tide, however, swept a bitter counter-current. Bethlehem also brought back sad memories. Naomi remembered the awful famine that forced her family to immi-grate to Moab. She remembered three Bethlehemites who were gone now—her husband and her sons. Bethlehem re-minded her of great joy—but also unforgettable heartbreak.

In their greeting, "Can this be Naomi?" the townspeople reminded her of her heartbreak. Even her own name had become a mockery.

In Hebrew thought, a name was more than just a personal identifier. It described a person's character and even forecast one's future! For example, Jacob meant "schemer" (Gen. 27:36). Ask poor Esau how appropriate that name was!

Similarly, the names Abraham ("father of many nations," Gen. 17:5-8) and Jesus ("Savior," Matt. 1:21) predicted their key roles in God's plan. A name change signaled a change in destiny—for example, when Jacob became Israel (Gen. 32:28) and Saul became Paul (Acts 13:9).

Now you can understand why Naomi exploded when the women said the word "Naomi." The name Naomi meant "lovely, pleasant." Her life had been anything but pleasant! Suddenly, the broken woman saw how her "pleasant" name clashed with her harsh, unpleasant destiny. She saw how her own name cruelly mocked her!

Bluntly, she rejected the women's question. "Don't call me 'Pleasant'!" she said. "Call me 'Bitter' (*mārā'*)! For the Al-mighty has made me very bitter" (Ruth 1:20, my translation of the Heb.).

Naomi blamed God for her disappointment. Her hopeful expectations bumped heads with harsh reality. That jolt shook Naomi and made her bitter. But what really galled her was God's role in her sorrow. She directly blamed God for her bitterness ("the Almighty has made my life very bitter"). She *expected* something of Him which clashed with what He actually had done.

What were her expectations? Perhaps she had expected God to end the famine quickly so her family could return home. Israel believed that food was God's provision (Ex. 16:8;

Ps. 136:25). He had placed Joseph in Egypt to feed Israel during famine (Gen. 45:5-8; 50:20). But no such provision had been made for Naomi. Or perhaps she expected God to protect her family. Certainly, He had protected Abraham while he lived on foreign soil (12:10-20; 20:1-18). Moab was no different than Egypt and Philistia.

Or perhaps she assumed that God would bless her family. They were all a part of God's blessed people, Israel. God had stopped Balaam's attempts to curse Israel in Moab (Num. 22–24). Certainly, God could bless her little family in that same land.

But the famine did not end soon, and Naomi's family died in Moab. Naomi believed that God had let her down. She had trusted that He would look out for them, but He had disappointed her. Her life was "bitter" not "pleasant," and she mockingly asked to be called "Bitter."

At times we all feel as if God has let us down. Some of us have prayed earnestly for the salvation of friends and family. But nothing has happened. Others of us lie racked with pain in hospital beds. Apparently, God has ignored our anguished cries for healing. Still others have tragically lost loved ones — spouses or children — in the prime of life. Down deep we agonize over why God failed to protect them.

Frankly, we are disappointed with God. At the same time, we hesitate to admit it either to ourselves or to God. We are much more timid and polite than Naomi. We just do not feel comfortable being as blunt with God as she was. We feel like saying, "Lord, You blew it! I'm mad at You!" But we cannot bring ourselves to do it.

After all, how can we criticize Someone who has been so generous? God has freed us from slavery to sin and showered us with many blessings. Without Him, we would be doomed to self-destruction. To be angry with Him sounds like crass ingratitude.

So, we blame ourselves rather than God. We tell ourselves, "It's really my fault. If I were more spiritual, I wouldn't feel this way about God." Or we appeal to the fact that God is perfect. We say, "God always does things perfectly — I must be the problem." We convince ourselves that something is wrong with us, not with God.

Here Naomi teaches us an important truth. It is all right to admit our disappointment with God. To do so is an expression of our faithfulness. It shows that we want an open, honest relationship with Him.

Indictment for Emptiness

In my local paper, ads appear regularly for weight-loss clinics. They use a common advertising device—the before and after approach. Two photographs of the same person stand side by side. The "before" picture shows the person very overweight, but the "after" frame shows him slimmer and more attractive. The clinic gets the credit for the startling change. The message is, "We can do this for you too! Just call us."

Naomi used the same before and after device to explain her outrage (Ruth 1:21). There was one difference, however. She looked worse in the "after" picture. The "before" snapshot was a happy one ("I went away full"). It certainly was full. There stood Naomi's whole family—she, Elimelech, Mahlon, and Kilion—on the day they left Bethlehem. Though hungry, they were happy.

But look how dreary the "after" picture is ("the Lord has brought me back empty"). It was certainly empty. There stood Naomi—alone except for Ruth—on the day she returned to Bethlehem. She looked pathetic—older, grayer, stooped, wrinkled. What an awful change! She was no advertisement for God's goodness!

Naomi had blamed God for her disappointment. Here she blamed Him for a second failure—deprivation. He had deprived her of her loved ones. In her eyes, He had committed highway robbery, stealing her treasures and leaving her empty. To strengthen the point, she added, "Why call me Naomi? The Lord has afflicted me; the Almighty has brought misfortune upon me."

Now notice something. Naomi did not make any excuses to get God off the hook. She did not gloss over things by saying, "Oh, well, that's the way life is sometimes." She also bypassed the popular theological solution of appealing to God's permissive will. She did not say, "God only permitted this to happen. He didn't really cause it."

And she sidestepped the most common excuse of all—she refused to blame herself. She did not say, "God is so good; I must have done something wrong." No, Naomi directly blamed God for her suffering. She bluntly claimed, "All this tragedy—God did it to me!"

What a startling statement! Its frankness takes us aback. Few of us speak about God with such boldness. Even fewer of us have the courage actually to blame God for anything. We all remember what happened to complainers in the Bible.

For murmuring against Him, God condemned Israel to die in the desert (Num. 14:21-23). And pity the poor sons of Korah. The ground opened up under their feet and swallowed them alive (16:31-33). We are all afraid of similar treatment—a lightning bolt or a sudden heart attack.

At the same time, we can question Naomi's fairness. She strikes some of us as a crybaby. Her philosophy seems to be a perversion of a well-known proverb: "It's not whether you win or lose but how you lay the blame." We wonder if she's passing the buck—blaming God for what may have been her responsibility.

Others offer different diagnoses. Some see Naomi's reaction as symptomatic of a deeper problem. They think her anger showed a flabby faith in God. They wonder why she did not invoke some of God's promises or whether her walk with the Lord was close. Still others read Naomi's reaction as simple rebellion. They believe that Naomi simply needed to submit her will to God and accept her God-given lot.

Naomi's outburst raises a crucial question. That question has nagged us from the story's very beginning: who is responsible for this tragedy? Is Naomi? Is God? The answer is simple: we do not know. This case is different from that of Job. The Book of Job traced Job's suffering to God Himself (see Job 1–2). The Book of Ruth, however, gives no explanation.

In the end, the women praised God for salvaging Naomi's

situation (Ruth 4:14). That might imply that the book credited God with responsibility for her circumstances, but we cannot be sure. We do not know how the book's author felt about Naomi's outcry.

Biblical Bluntness

One thing needs to be said in Naomi's defense. The Bible models a surprising frankness in the way God's people talk to Him. Examples of this biblical bluntness abound. Recall Moses' intercession with God over murmuring Israel (Num. 14). God had decided to kill off Israel and start a new chosen people with Moses (v. 12). But Moses boldly appealed to God's personal pride.

He argued (vv. 13-16), "Lord, You can't do that. You'll be the laughingstock of the nations. They'll accuse You of a giant coverup: You buried Israel in the desert because You couldn't deliver on Your promises." What amazing frankness with God! What transparency before God! Even more amazing, the argument worked. God decided to let the younger generation enter the Promised Land (vv. 20-24).

Consider also the Prophet Jeremiah. He faithfully preached to Judah but with little success. Indeed, the people plotted to get rid of him. Finally, he could not stand things anymore. He bluntly accused God of shady dealings with him. Jeremiah claimed God had tricked and bullied him into becoming a prophet. He said, "O Lord, You deceived me, and I was deceived; You overpowered me and prevailed" (Jer. 20:7). In utter despair, he cried, "Cursed be the day I was born!" (v. 14)

Again, Jeremiah showed a startling bluntness with God. Like Moses, he let his true feelings show. He opted for transparency before God. The psalmists practiced the same kind of transparency. Naomi's pained outcry followed that pattern of biblical bluntness.

But why does the Bible encourage, not discourage, such directness? We tend to view it as borderline belief if not outright unbelief. I suggest that the Bible views such frankness as an expression of genuine faithfulness to God. First, it lives out a simple, biblical truth: God knows all our thoughts and feelings (Ps. 139:1-4; Jer. 20:12).

There is no point in taking the cuttlefish approach. We cannot hide our inner emotions from God's searching eyes and ears. So, we might as well talk them over with God. We might as well put our relationship with God on an honest footing. He knows what is going on already. By being transparent, we treat God as a friend who loves us, not a foe who threatens us.

Second, transparency shows that we truly trust God. It says, "I know, Lord, that You love me as I am—warts and all." Indeed, it pays God the ultimate compliment.

My wife, Pam, first taught me this truth. I have always found it difficult to share emotions, especially anger. My own upbringing discouraged such frankness. So I assumed that conflicts would eventually either work themselves out or blow away. I became an expert cuttlefish!

As a result, after marriage I found it difficult to reveal my feelings to my wife. I would hide them, waiting for the right moment to bring up a painful subject. Finally, after I shared some long-held feelings, Pam said, "You know, Bob, it's no compliment that you're so afraid of me. How can our relationship grow if you don't tell me about the things that are bothering you?"

The truth hit me like a ton of bricks. She was right. By hiding I had treated her as if she were an awful ogre, not a loving wife. Further, I had robbed our marriage of material for growth. How could we grow closer if I withheld things from her?

It is the same way with God. Naomi, the psalmists, Job, and Jeremiah model such transparency. To hide from Him is no compliment to Him. It says, "I'm sorry, Lord, You're such a hothead that I can't risk Your reaction." On the other hand, to be transparent with Him says, "Lord, I trust You enough to risk my feelings with You."

That is true faithfulness. It relieves us of the burden of hiding. It also gives our relationship with God a chance to grow. It gives it an honest basis.

Out from Hiding

Growing up, one of my favorite television programs was "The Lone Ranger." Each week, he and his Indian sidekick, Tonto, faithfully battled injustice in the old West. Of course, no one knew who the Lone Ranger really was. He always hid his identity behind a black mask. And every show ended with the same closing lines:

"Say, who was that masked man?" someone would ask.

"Don't you know who that is?" a smiling friend would reply. "He's the Lone Ranger!"

You may be hiding behind a mask. You may be afraid that people will discover who you really are. You may fear that they will reject you if they find out. You may wonder if even God can love you with your anger or bitterness. That is where Naomi's outburst points you in the right direction. She models the openness before God which truly pleases Him. She shows that, since He knows us anyway, we might as well treat Him as if He does.

It is time to remove the mask. It is time to step from behind the camouflage. I suggest three steps to do this. First, I recommend a no-holds barred, blunt prayertime alone with God. That sounds more frightening than it is. Remember, in the Bible God honored all those who talked straight with Him. The experience may be a new one for you, but it is worth the risk. In such a prayer, I suggest that you let God know exactly where you are. In contemporary terms, "Let Him have it."

Second, I advise you to share your prayer experience in church. Select an occasion where you feel comfortable. It could be with your small group Bible study, at Wednesday prayer meeting, or during a period of congregational sharing. You need not go into all the details. Simply summarize your experience. I know you will feel great relief.

Finally, I suggest that you talk to God frankly in the future. Make transparency a habit. Keep the mask off permanently. Remember: transparency pays God the ultimate compliment. It shows that you really trust Him. It is an act of faithfulness.

Chapter Six

Provision: Faithfulness Meets Needs

Ruth 2:1-17

Bill and Mary were a fine young Christian couple. My wife and I got to know them while Bill was studying at our seminary. They were preparing to go to the mission field. But they were not prepared for what lay ahead.

After graduation, Bill and Mary left our area to raise their missionary support. We eagerly followed their progress through periodic prayer letters. Sometime later, I met them for lunch during a short visit to their area. Sadly, I found them struggling with discouragement. Financial support was coming in at a snail's pace. They were even having trouble getting opportunities to share their burden for Europe.

Worse, they were not making enough money, so they both had to get jobs. That put them in a real bind. It left them with less time and energy for their primary ministry. They began to wonder whether God really wanted them on the mission field. He had not provided their needs. At least, not yet.

Their problem is a common one. The Bible records many examples of people who waited for God to provide. All they had was His spoken word. For example, Abraham migrated to a strange, distant land with nothing in hand but God's spoken promise (Gen. 12:1-3). When Moses asked the Egyptian Pharaoh for Israel's freedom, his only backing was God's promise of deliverance (Ex. 3-5).

Joshua took on the mighty Canaanite cities. His only weapon was God's assurance of victory (Josh. 1). In despair, barren Hannah tearfully asked God for a child. Her only hope was Eli's word that God had heard her prayer (1 Sam. 1:10-11, 17). Jesus' disciples scattered to preach the Gospel across the world. Their only confidence was the "Lo, I am with you always" given them by Jesus (Matt. 28:20, KJV).

Every church has Christians awaiting God's provision for similar crises. There are young single parents with only minimal job skills struggling to hold a steady job, feed their little families, and pay the light bill. There are older people who have just lost their lifelong companion and are desperately lonely. How will they survive such brokenheartedness? All look to God to get them through.

Life's crises are many. Accidents disable the strong. Unemployment makes families unstable. Disease steals one's health. Divorce shatters hearts and dreams. Death breaks up a tight family circle. The question is, will God provide in such situations? The victims have served God faithfully. Faithfulness to Him is still their aim. But is God dependable? Will He honor their faithfulness? Will He truly provide their needs?

The opening scene of Ruth 2 answers, "Yes!" It shows that God provides for those who faithfully live for Him. It also shows the kind of faithfulness which pleases God. Here Ruth and Boaz are our examples.

Bold Faithfulness

A crisis for Naomi and Ruth lurked behind this scene. They had to get food for themselves. By God's grace, the land had food again (Ruth 1:6). And providentially, they had arrived just as the barley harvest began, probably late April (v. 22). Food was available in quantity. Their problem was how to get some of it.

They had not planted a crop of their own, so they had no field to harvest. And they could not simply help themselves to someone else's crop. That would be robbery! Amid prosperity, cruel poverty still stalked them.

At the same time, they had little time to waste. In 1908, archeologists found a tablet at Gezer with an agricultural calendar inscribed on it. This Gezer Calendar illumines the background of Ruth. It reads:

"Month of barley harvest.
Month when everything [else] is harvested."[3]

In other words, in Israel the entire harvest season lasted only two months. Around Bethlehem only the wheat harvest followed that of barley (see Ruth 2:23). That meant that Naomi and Ruth had only two months to act.

Surprisingly, Ruth proposed a solution. She told Naomi, "Let me go to the fields and pick up the leftover grain behind anyone in whose eyes I find favor" (v. 2). In Hebrew, the statement is not a request for permission but a declaration of Ruth's intention.

Ruth's sudden show of initiative so soon after her arrival in Bethlehem is striking. One wonders where Ruth got the idea. Did she know that Israelite custom permitted it? And what about Naomi's passivity? Was she too old to work or just too depressed to do anything? Why didn't she contact relatives for help? Whatever the reason, Ruth seized the opportunity which the opening of the harvest offered.

She aimed to take advantage of an Israelite custom called gleaning. To glean is to pick up grain, olives, or grapes left behind by reapers. The Law of Moses made this practice legal in Israel (see Lev. 19:9-10; 23:22; Deut. 24:19-22). The Israelites recognized that God actually owned the land, and they were only His tenants. The custom of gleaning was the way God provided food for the poor in the land.

One should not envy the life of gleaners, however. Gleaning probably only provided the poor with basic subsistence. In modern terms, it amounted to living off the money that could be obtained by the collection of aluminum cans. Further, though backed by Law, the custom depended on the goodwill of landowners and reapers.

Greed may have led many to ignore the Law. That may be one reason why the prophets later preached against Israel's abuse of the poor (Isa. 1:16-17; Amos 2:7). In sum, Ruth's proposed venture would be no picnic in the countryside!

In 1911, Norwegian novelist and college professor Ole E. Rölvaag addressed a group of immigrants in Minnesota. He commented on his own experience as an immigrant. For him, the greatest suffering was the loss of belonging. He said, "We have become strangers, strangers to the people we forsook, and strangers to the people we came to" (quoted by Maldwyn A. Jones, *Destination America*, New York: Holt, Rinehart and Winston, 1976, p. 240).

Ruth also faced that lack of belonging. Ruth was not only poor but also foreign. Israel viewed her as a Moabite—a stranger to be watched carefully. That may be why Ruth sought to follow someone "in whose eyes I find favor." She hoped to find a friendly, compassionate Israelite; someone who might look past her poverty and parentage and treat her kindly.

This leads to an important observation. Ruth's plan put her earlier commitment to Naomi into practice. She "walked her talk." Ruth was not satisfied with only saying great things. She and Naomi needed food to survive. They could not eat her words! No, Ruth put into action the devotion she had declared. She went to get food.

In doing so, she took several risks. As an outsider, she risked an icy reception by Israelite field hands. She might even have been physically abused or thrown out of the field. Ruth models the kind of commitment discussed in the last chapter. Faithfulness which pleases God carries out its commitments.

She also reminds us of what it means to follow Jesus faithfully. It is one thing to sing "I have decided to follow Jesus." It is another to share the Gospel with an unsaved friend. It is nice to sing "Let the beauty of Jesus be seen in me." It is another to be kind to a drunk on the street. It is easy to sing "Take my life and let it be." It is another to visit prisoners in jail. It is fine to sing "Wherever He leads I'll go." It is another to cook meals for a sick neighbor.

What Ruth said, she did. Jesus expects us to do the same—in ordinary, practical ways.

Her Lucky Day

Ruth went to glean in the fields (Ruth 2:3). Where were the fields and what were they like? Apparently, they were somewhere below the city of Bethlehem. Literally, the Hebrew text says that she "went down" to reach them. Bethlehem sits on the eastern ridge of Israel's central mountain range. Below lie the sloping Judean hills which fade into the barren wilderness along the Dead Sea.

We cannot be certain, but the fields may have been downhill east of the city. This is the same area where the angels later announced Jesus' birth (Luke 2:8-14).

Further, the farmland was divided into individual "fields" each owned by a different resident of Bethlehem. Probably, there were no visible boundary lines or markers to identify a specific field. The area may have resembled a patchwork quilt—separate fields in odd shapes and sizes.

Now two important things happened in the fields that day. First, there was a remarkable coincidence, perhaps even a stroke of good luck. Just by chance, Ruth chose a field which belonged to a man named Boaz (v. 3). Given the patchwork of fields, to find that field was pure luck. Ruth did not even know Boaz yet. But even if Ruth had, she would have had no way to know which field was his.

Then, again by chance, Boaz happened to visit that very field shortly after Ruth arrived (vv. 4-5). The situation was set up for Ruth and Boaz to meet. Now we must ask, "Was this really a coincidence?" The book's author pricked our curiosity by the way he vaguely commented, "As it turned out." Ruth found herself in Boaz's field (v. 3). Then he opened verse 4 with, literally, "And behold, Boaz came." The author was obviously understating his case.

I must confess to having used the technique once myself. One night I took a different route home from church. When my kids asked about the change, I lamely explained that I wanted to see some different scenery. Just then, I pulled into the lot of our favorite ice cream parlor. Faking surprise, I said, "Well, how about that! The car stopped here all by itself!" My kids quickly saw through the trick. "Oh, sure,

Provision

Dad!" they scoffed, heading for the shop. By exaggerating the "accidental" nature of our stop, I gave away the fact that I had planned it all along.

I think that is what the writer in Ruth did. By stressing Ruth's "good luck," he hinted that, in fact, God had planned things. God's invisible hand had guided the "accidental" meeting of Ruth and Boaz. Mere coincidence was actually divine providence.

But who was this new character, Boaz? Verse 1 introduced him as a friend of Naomi's and a relative of Elimelech. (Some Bible translations call him a relative of Naomi.) Perhaps he was among the family she came to know when she married Elimelech.

More important, Boaz was a "man of standing." In Hebrew, this phrase was a colorful expression. Literally, it meant "mighty man of power." In Israel, "power" could mean physical strength (2 Sam. 22:33, 40), personal ability (1 Kings 11:28), or wealth (2 Kings 15:20). Apparently, Boaz was a powerful person—someone whose wealth and good reputation gave him influence in Bethlehem. Later Boaz praised Ruth's character with a similar expression (see Ruth 3:11).

There is something else striking about this remarkable coincidence. Ruth went looking for favor (Ruth 2:2) and bumped into Boaz. Boaz was just the person to give it! If Ruth and Naomi needed help, knowing Boaz would certainly come in handy.

He was a relative, and he carried clout in town. On the other hand, the women may have been unsure of his response to a Moabitess in his field.

This remarkable coincidence conveys an important message. We all often live like skeptics. Like the disciple Thomas (John 20:25), we follow the advice of a popular proverb, "Seeing is believing." Here, however, the Bible reminds us that God is at work in our lives even when we do not see Him. We would do well to look closely at "chance" events in our lives. We might find the Lord Himself working in the shadows behind them.

The Meeting

Apparently, Boaz noticed Ruth. He asked his foreman about her. "She is the young Moabitess who came back from Moab with Naomi," the man replied. Then he summarized her activities since she arrived on the scene—her request for permission to glean and her diligent labor all morning (Ruth 2:5-7).

By calling her "the young Moabitess who came back," the man revealed that Ruth was already well-known in Bethlehem. That is no surprise. The town was fairly small and probably had few—if any—other Moabites.

This brings us to the day's second big event. For a tense moment, Boaz and Ruth probably glanced at each other silently. This was Ruth's moment of truth. How would Boaz respond to a Moabitess? Would he speak to her or ignore her? Israel and Moab certainly were not the best of friends. Moab even worshiped a false god. If he did speak, would he offer her a warm welcome or angrily throw her out?

Whew! He not only spoke—he showed her favor! During the rest of the long day, he graciously granted her more than she could have dreamed (vv. 8-14). First, he gave her the *permission* she asked for (v. 7). But beyond her request, he insisted that she work only in his field:

> My daughter, listen to me. Don't go and glean in another field and don't go away from here. Stay here with my servant girls. Watch the field where the men are harvesting, and follow along after the girls (vv. 8-9).

Notice how emphatically he insisted that Ruth work in his field. He used three sentences to say the same thing—"Stay here!"

Second, he gave her *protection*. He promised that the men would not touch her (v. 9; see also vv. 15-16, 22). We do not know what concerned Boaz. Perhaps he thought his workers might verbally abuse her. They might take offense at her being both a Moabitess and a gleaner. Perhaps he worried that a few overly loyal workers might protect his harvest

70

from her. They might rough her up if she strayed from where gleaners normally worked.

Whatever the case, Boaz put his workers on notice: Ruth was a favorite of the boss. Like his permission, the protection Boaz provided exceeded Ruth's original request.

Finally, he gave her *provision*. He provided her with water. Whenever she got thirsty, he instructed her to drink from the company water cooler (v. 9). Field work was hot, sweaty business. The sun showed field hands no mercy. Its heat beat down on them all day long. So Boaz had several workers maintain a large jug of water for his employees. He gave Ruth permission to ease her thirst from that jug. Again, this exceeded Ruth's earlier request.

Boaz also invited her to the company lunch (v. 14). Amazingly, he himself—not just a servant—served her some roasted grain. To be served by the boss was a gesture of great honor. One can only imagine what the other workers thought about that. In fact, what did Ruth herself think? She had come as a poor gleaner and ended up as the boss' guest of honor. Talk about "finding favor"! Unexpectedly, she had struck a bonanza!

But the best was yet to come. When Ruth got up to glean, Boaz turned to his employees and issued some more instructions (vv. 15-16). He told them what he had already told Ruth (vv. 8-9). They were to allow Ruth to glean even in an area usually off-limits to gleaners. Normally, gleaners worked among the standing stalks, picking up dropped grain. Ruth was permitted to glean among the piles of cut sheaves. The other workers were not to embarrass or rebuke her.

But Boaz added a bonus—a real surprise! He ordered them to "pull out some stalks for her from the bundles and leave them for her to pick up" (v. 16). Ruth would not have the slim pickings of ordinary gleaning. Boaz made sure that she would have plenty to gather. Again, he went far beyond Ruth's original request. Indeed, such generosity probably would have struck ancient Israelites as unheard-of.

Here Boaz models another dimension of faithfulness: he was generous to those in need. He bypassed the letter of the

Mosaic Law to obey its spirit. The Law required him merely to make gleaning possible. His permission simply met that requirement.

His protection and extraordinary provision, however, came from a heart grateful to God. He knew that God had been generous to him. He knew that God delights in those who care for the poor. So he pleased his Lord by sharing with Ruth some of what he owned.

I am not very mechanical. Over the years, I have learned to make some simple repairs to save money. Recently, however, as I braked to a stop arriving at work, I noticed a disturbing grinding noise. A knowledgeable friend diagnosed the problem as worn-out brake pads. As I removed the noisy wheel for closer inspection, a student on his way home joined me.

The timing of his arrival was right because I was not sure what to do next. Without fanfare, he spent several hours replacing the pads on my front brakes. I know he was headed home to study, but he willingly helped me get my car going again. He was generous with what he had to give—his mechanical skills.

That student was my Boaz. He saw my need and gave of what he had. Now let me ask, what do you and I have to share? Some of us have more money than time. Boaz reminds us to share with those in need. Others of us have more time than money. We can share that with others too. We can care for a neighbor's children, visit shut-ins, or give rides to those who cannot drive. We can read to the blind, cook meals for the sick, or tutor kids having trouble in school.

Still others have hands-on, "fix-it" skills. We can help others who cannot afford to hire such experts. We can unstop a sink, tile a floor, wire a lamp, repair a screen, or fix a car. Others have more professional skills—lawyers, doctors, nurses, counselors. We too can share our expertise with the needy.

As I wrote these words, a phone call—and an opportunity to be generous—interrupted my work. A missionary group was preparing Bibles to send to a communist country at

Christmas. They needed someone who knew Hebrew to answer a few questions about their translation. At first, I resisted the intrusion. A subtle "Don't-bother-me" crossed my mind. Then I realized—here was my chance to live out this lesson. Here was my chance to be generous with what I had.

So I took the time, opened my Hebrew Bible, and answered their questions. That is what pleases God—using whatever we have to help others in need. To do that is to "walk" our "talk," to give feet to our faith. That is what Boaz did for Ruth. Faced with a needy situation, we must ask ourselves, what do I have to share?

God's Faithfulness

Why did Boaz treat Ruth so kindly? You may have your own hunches. Was Boaz simply generous by temperament? If so, such kindness came very naturally to him. Or, had he heard the voice of duty? Had his conscience gently reminded him that such giving pleased God? Or, maybe Boaz worried about his civic reputation. People might think less of him if he did not help her. Or, had Boaz fallen in love with Ruth? Did his attention have romantic aims?

Apparently, his kindness surprised even Ruth. She fell on her face to the ground—a typical oriental gesture of humility. She asked, "Why have I found such favor in your eyes that you notice me—a foreigner?" (Ruth 2:10) For added emphasis, she used a clever wordplay.

In Hebrew, the words "notice" and "foreigner" sound alike and may even be related. Elsewhere the word "notice" described the recognition of someone already familiar, not of a stranger (Gen. 37:33; 1 Kings 18:7). By contrast, "foreigner" always referred to someone or something unfamiliar—a non-Israelite (2 Sam. 15:19) or nonfamily member (Job 19:15). So, through the pun, Ruth asked, "Why have you *noticed* the *unnoticed?*" In other words, she wanted to know why, though she was a total stranger to Boaz, he had treated her as if he already knew her.

Boaz confirmed her suspicions. He, indeed, already knew about her: "I've been told all about what you have done for your mother-in-law since the death of your husband—how you left your father and mother and your homeland and came to live with a people you did not know before" (v. 11). Boaz had heard the word going around town about Ruth. She had a very good reputation. The town greatly admired her self-sacrifice—she had left her family and native land forever. She had settled down among total strangers.

On the plus side, she probably faced no great language barrier. Ancient Moabite and ancient Hebrew were sister languages—about as close as Spanish and Portuguese. On the other hand, she was back in kindergarten when it came to knowing Israel. She would have to learn her ABCs in Israel's religion and customs. That is why Boaz was so generous: he honored Ruth's devotion to Naomi.

Finally, Boaz wished Ruth something very special. Indeed, verse 12 is one of the most important verses in the whole book. He said, "May the Lord repay you for what you have done. May you be richly rewarded by the Lord, the God of Israel, under whose wings you have come to take refuge." Boaz sounded like an employer. He talked in ancient "paycheck" language. (Now he's talking our language!) In Hebrew, the second line, "richly rewarded," literally meant "may your wages be paid in full." Genesis used the same word for the wages which Laban was to have paid Jacob (Gen. 29:15; 31:7, 41).

Boaz said that, like Jacob, Ruth had earned wages for her labor. Ruth's labor was her devotion to Naomi (Ruth 2:11) and to God ("under whose wings," v. 12). Thus, Boaz prayed that Ruth would soon get a big paycheck from God—she had earned it!

Now this may make us a little uneasy. It sounds like works righteousness. Actually, it should remind us of one aspect of God's grace. It recalls that God likes to reward people who please Him. Job 34:11 summarized this important biblical truth: "He [God] repays a man for what he has done; He brings upon him what his conduct deserves" (see also Ps. 28:4; Jer. 25:14).

One who does evil receives evil wages, one who does well,

good wages. The same idea lies behind the Beatitudes of Jesus (Matt. 5:1-12). Jesus also taught that deeds done without show earn God's reward (6:1-4).

But how is that different from earning God's favor by good works? The difference is this: the Bible teaches that God *may* reward us, not that He *must* reward us. Our good deeds put Him under no obligation to repay us. In fact, we owe Him everything; He owes us nothing. However good we are, God still is free to do as He pleases—to reward or not reward.

More important, the Bible stresses that there is only one reason God is ever good to us—His grace. All our good deeds still amount to a pile of filthy rags beside His scale of righteousness (Isa. 64:6). In fact, we are so sinful that there is no human way to make up for our evil. Jesus died for us because we could not satisfy God's standard of perfect righteousness.

At the same time, the teaching about reward reminds us of something important about God. He is a gracious, compassionate God. He loves to be generous toward those who delight Him. Like a good father, He loves to do nice things for His children. He rewards children who please Him out of the goodness of His heart.

Ruth's Reward

Ruth experienced that herself. When the workday ended, "she threshed [lit., beat out] the barley she had gathered" (Ruth 2:17). In other words, she pounded the grain with a curved stick or wooden hammer. This would separate the husks from the kernel and lighten the load to carry home.

But notice how much she collected that day—"about an ephah of barley." An ephah amounted to about a half bushel—about 29 (U.S.) pounds. That was an amazing amount for one day's work. At the ancient Mesopotamian city of Mari, workers earned about 1–2 pounds per day. So, Ruth had earned half a month's wages in a single day. Apparently, the reapers had obeyed Boaz's orders! Ruth had, indeed, found the favor she sought.

More important, God had rewarded her faithfulness as Boaz said (v. 12). Through Boaz's generosity, God provided food for Ruth and Naomi. And plenty of it! Ruth's experience reminds us of a biblical truth: God rewards faithfulness by providing for needs. As Paul taught, He is a good provider: "And my God will meet all your needs according to His glorious riches in Christ Jesus" (Phil. 4:19).

Conclusion

A year passed after my first visit with my missionary friends, Bill and Mary. During another visit in their area, I shared breakfast with Bill. What a happy change I found! Joy had replaced discouragement. Watching their son grow was a delight, and Mary was expecting their second child. To support them, Bill had to work as a prison chaplain while they continued to raise their missionary support.

The job proved to be a blessing in disguise from God. Besides providing for their needs, Bill found the experience spiritually challenging and rewarding. He had learned much about hurting people. And he had touched many of their lives with the Gospel. Most important, the couple had finally raised all their support. They could now arrange their departure for the mission field. They learned the lesson of Ruth and Naomi: God provides the needs of those who are faithful to Him.

Samuel Zwemer, a pioneer missionary among Muslims, once remarked that he lived "from hand to mouth." Fortunately, he added, while the mouth was his, the hand was the Lord's. God had always provided.

Whatever your need, you can count on the same provision. God delights to reward your faithfulness. Your task is to wait patiently until God's provision shows itself.

At the same time, like Boaz, you may be God's means of provision. He may use your generosity—whether in time or talent—to meet someone else's needs. And then you too may receive His gracious reward!

Chapter Seven

Gratitude: Faithfulness
Gives Thanks
Ruth 2:18-23

Normally, it is not polite to read someone else's mail. In fact, such snooping is against the law. It's an invasion of privacy and carries some severe penalties. Every year, however, a postal service employee breaks the law again and again. One year, in doing so, she learned something important.

She works at the Dead Letter Office in Washington, D.C. Her job is to read all the mail addressed to Santa Claus. Local post offices collect Santa's mail and forward it to Washington. Can you imagine reading all those children's Christmas lists!

After one particular Christmas, the worker suddenly realized something was wrong. In the months before Christmas, Santa had received thousands of letters from children asking for things. In the months after Christmas, however, only one child bothered to send a card thanking him.

How true of us. Greed comes more easily than gratitude. We are quick to ask but slow to say thanks. We easily list our wishes but find it hard to give credit. We hurry to seek favors but are slow as snails in showing appreciation. We readily render requests but grudgingly give gratitude.

Jesus saw this problem long ago. En route to Jerusalem one day, He met ten lepers in a northern village. They asked for mercy, and He miraculously healed them. But only one—a Samaritan, at that—came back to thank Jesus (Luke 17:11-19). Recall Jesus' sad, memorable words: "Were not all ten

77

cleansed? Where are the other nine? Was no one found to return and give praise to God except this foreigner?" (vv. 17-18)

Sadly, we so often find ourselves among the ungrateful nine. Our ingratitude may have several causes. We may be embarrassed by someone's generosity. We may feel unworthy of such attention. This is especially true if the gift is out of proportion to the depth of our friendship.

Picture yourself at a birthday party in your honor. Someone from work gives you a gorgeous leather jacket. The other guests gasp—it has "expensive" written all over it. But suppose you hardly know the giver. You feel embarrassed. You wonder what expectations the giver may have of you. You worry about your ability to meet them. Is the person trying to buy your friendship?

The need for acceptance may encourage ingratitude. Some of us see gifts as a kind of money. We think they measure how much our family and friends value us. Costly gifts confirm that we are worth something to them, cheap ones that we are worthless. It is hard to say "thanks" for a gift that seems like small change left for a sloppy waitress. Our feelings of rejection produce ingratitude.

Some people feel gifts impose on them a debt they must repay. They cannot simply accept a gift, something given without strings attached. They feel they "owe" the giver a gift of similar value. So, they carefully calculate each gift's worth and keep records of who gave it. Soon they come to resent getting any gifts at all. And it is hard to say "thanks" when one feels so trapped!

Pride causes ingratitude in some people. They feel very worthy of receiving generosity. They too keep careful records—but of all the things they have done for others. They expect to be repaid properly. Sadly, such pride is doomed to disappointment. Few friends can satisfy their expectations. When no proper repayment comes, they feel cheated. And robbery victims rarely return a genuine "Thank you"!

This brings us to Naomi and Ruth. As we saw, Boaz had

just handed them a bonanza. He had shown Ruth special favor. The pile of grain gleaned that day was clear proof. And the harvest had just started! But how did Naomi and Ruth respond to the generosity of Boaz?

The two widows will remind us that gratitude is one way to live out faithfulness to God. A faithful Christian says "thanks" to God for His generosity.

Surprise — Leftovers!

Dusk had fallen on Bethlehem. The sun had snugly settled behind the western hills. Murky shadows shrouded the eastern slope where Ruth probably worked. All alone Ruth packed up for home. Presumably, following ancient custom, she spread her shawl on the ground, piled the grain in it, and put the bundle over her shoulder or on her head. Then she trudged up the hill to town (Ruth 2:18).

Undoubtedly, Naomi anxiously awaited her. She probably had not had a very easy day! I imagine that her thoughts never left Ruth. She wondered how the day was going. Had Ruth been well received? Were the workers treating her kindly? Perhaps she offered an occasional prayer for Ruth's success.

As the day wore on, fear wrestled with faith. At the onset of dusk, the struggle grew even worse. Naomi worried whether Ruth had found any kindness. Had the harvesters aided or abused her? Would Ruth bring food home tonight or come home empty-handed? Or—would she come home at all? Nervously, Naomi paced the floor waiting for the shuffle of footsteps in the street and the squeak of the front door.

Soon Ruth arrived. Naomi could hardly believe her eyes! Immediately, she saw how much grain Ruth had gathered (v. 18). She knew that gleaners never brought home that much grain in one day. Something unusual had happened on the field. Swelling excitement swept her fears out the door.

Without speaking, Ruth surprised Naomi again. She handed her not just raw grain freshly gleaned, but food already cooked. Normally, gleaners do not come home with cooked food. Where had she gotten it? Recall that Boaz had invited

Ruth to lunch that day (v. 14). He had even served her himself—a great honor. Remember also that the serving was so generous that Ruth "ate all she wanted and had some left over."

The food's reappearance here surprised us too. The Bible said nothing about what happened to the leftovers until now. To see their significance, however, we need to go back to the field for a moment and observe something important.

Ruth might have done one of several things with the food. She could have simply left it uneaten where she sat. Or she might have eaten it herself before coming home. She had worked hard all day gleaning and threshing. She was probably hungry. A snack of leftovers would have fortified her for the long climb up the hill. To carry the large load of grain home would have certainly required strength. No one could have criticized her for eating it. No one even knew she had it.

Instead, Ruth shared the food with Naomi. Apparently, she had tucked it away in an ancient doggie bag, probably a pocket or large fold in her clothes. Now back home, she gave the food to Naomi. We cannot be sure, but it may have been the only food Naomi had that day, maybe even for several days. Ruth's gesture shows us the first way to show gratitude: to share the gifts we have with someone else.

We all face this possibility. God has showered us with generous gifts too. We must decide what we will do with them. God has gifted some of us with physical strength. We actually thrive on hard work. Will we share that gift with the weak? Will we help a handicapped person get to church? Will we lift heavy loads for an elderly person?

God has given others great emotional empathy. People tell us that talks with us encourage them. Will we carve out time to listen to their pain? Will we make ourselves available to say, "I'm sorry you're hurting so much." Still others have talents—organizational, musical, artistic, practical. Will we dedicate them to God's service? Will we find ways to use them for other people?

Whatever our gifts, to share them with others is to show gratitude to God that we have them. It is to say "thanks!" for

His goodness. It is to live out our faithfulness practically.

Thankful Praise

As we saw, the amount of grain and the leftovers excited Naomi. Her heart pounded wildly, her face beamed with joy. She knew that something special had happened to Ruth. She could hardly wait for an explanation. Finally, in her excited curiosity, she blurted out two rapid-fire questions (Ruth 2:19). They showed Naomi's astonishment. In modern paraphrase, she asked, "Where on earth did you work today?"

Before Ruth could answer, however, Naomi added something. She gave thanks for her benefactor. Without knowing his identity, she exclaimed: "Blessed be the man who took notice of you!" (v. 19) In the Old Testament, such blessings conveyed two things. On the one hand, they indirectly asked God to treat the other person well because of the generosity shown. Most of them said; "May such-and-such be blessed by the Lord" (see v. 20).

Specifically, they requested God to give him "blessing"— that is, prosperity. In this case, Naomi may even have had the truth that is expressed in Proverbs 22:9 in mind: "A generous man will himself be blessed, for he shares his food with the poor." If so, she asked God actually to implement that proverb. On the other hand, such blessings expressed simple, joyful gratitude for something good. Paraphrased, they meant, "How wonderful! I'm so grateful!"

Now this is significant. So far, Naomi did not know who the person was. She had no idea whether the generosity came with "strings attached." Was the giver a sleazy conniver? Had he exacted some sort of "deal" from poor Ruth—cooking or cleaning in exchange for grain? Was there some "price" to pay—sexual favors, even marriage, to gain the grain? Naomi did not know.

In fact, she did not need such details. She was simply very thankful! She thanked God for the grain gift, regardless of how it came about. Thus, she models another important aspect of faithfulness—a grateful heart whatever the circumstances.

In her best-selling book *The Hiding Place,* Corrie ten Boom illustrates this attitude. During World War II, the Germans imprisoned her and her sister, Betsie, for hiding Jews in their home in Holland. Corrie tells about moving into new, flea-infested barracks at Ravensbruck.

"Betsie," Corrie protested, "how can we live in such a place!" In reply, Betsie recalled the Bible verse they had read that very morning: "Give thanks in all circumstances" (1 Thes. 5:18). She then led a reluctant Corrie in thanking God for everything—even the fleas!

Later, the two decided to risk holding a worship service each night. At first, they did so timidly for fear of the guards. Gradually, they became more bold, adding a second service to accommodate the large crowds coming. But something puzzled the two women. They had a strange freedom. The guards were everywhere, but none ever disrupted their worship. Why? Later they learned the reason: the guards avoided the place because of the fleas!

Wrote Corrie: "My mind rushed back to our first hour in this place. I remembered Betsie's bowed head, remembered her thanks to God for creatures I could see no use for."[4] Betsie was right to give thanks for the fleas. Through them, God provided what Corrie called "the sanctuary of God's fleas." Similarly, Naomi was ignorant of God's larger purposes. Like Betsie and Corrie, however, she faithfully gave thanks for God's gift.

What are your "fleas"? It may be a difficult boss at work or a rebellious child. It may be a cranky neighbor or a creaky house. It may be a lingering illness or an awful tragedy. Whatever it is, Naomi reminds us that faithfulness means to give thanks. We never know what God may be doing in our uncertain, even painful, circumstances. What pleases Him is for us to "give thanks in all circumstances."

Grateful Prayer

Finally, Ruth answered Naomi's question. "The name of the man I worked with today is Boaz" (Ruth 2:19). This sentence may reflect a little playfulness by Ruth. Notice two things.

First, Ruth might have mentioned the name first ("Boaz was the man's name"). Instead, she withheld it until the end of the line.

Second, a short, simple sentence would have been enough to answer Naomi. Instead, Ruth prefaced the name with a long, wordy sentence. I think Ruth wanted to prolong Naomi's joyous excitement. So she delayed saying the name "Boaz" until the very last moment.

This led to Naomi's second response of gratitude—Naomi prayed for Boaz. She said, "May he be blessed of the Lord who has not withdrawn His kindness to the living and to the dead" (v. 20, NASB). As with verse 19, Naomi once again prayed that God would bless Boaz.

Further, she gave the reason for asking this—Boaz's "kindness" (Heb. *hesed*). Naomi believed that his kindness merited a reward from God because such acts pleased God. Remember that God's reward for acts of *hesed* play a prominent role in the book. Naomi had prayed a similar prayer for Orpah and Ruth (1:8). Boaz had also said something similar to Ruth (2:12).

But notice something else about this prayer. In form, it was a blessing like the one in verse 19. Like the latter, it served a double purpose. It expressed gratitude to Boaz for his kindness to Ruth—paraphrased, "Oh, thank you so much, Boaz!"

At the same time, it asked God to reward Boaz. Literally, the prayer said, "May he be blessed [i.e., praised] to Yahweh." In essence, it commended Boaz to God for praise. It was a letter of commendation about Boaz sent to God in prayer.

All good organizations present special commendations for good work. Probably you have witnessed a presentation at your office, shop, or volunteer agency. You may even have received one yourself. They are given because a supervisor recommends someone for an award. The organization then presents the honoree with a plaque, medal, certificate, or gift.

One such ceremony took place on September 5, 1986 in Washington, D.C. The Marine Corps Commandant, General

P.X. Kelley, presented the Silver Star for gallantry in combat to retired Marine Sergeant Thomas E. Butt. Interestingly, the award came nearly twenty years after Butt's heroism in Vietnam. Butt knew that he had been recommended but that the original paperwork somehow was lost.

In 1985, as a gift to his father, Butt's sixteen-year-old son, Michael, contacted the Marine Corps about the award. Though sympathetic, the Corps said, "No paperwork, no award." Through persistence, however, Mike found the officer who had written the original citation. The man gladly wrote up Sergeant Butt again for bravery. Nearly two decades later, Tom Butt received the award he deserved. It was the recommendation that made the difference (M. McConnell, "Forever Proud," *Reader's Digest* 133 [Nov. 1988], 65–70).

Now Naomi's prayer for Boaz was just like that commendation. Paraphrased, it said, "Lord, let me call to Your attention something this man Boaz did. You really ought to do something special for him."

Here Naomi shows us the second way to express gratitude: commend someone to God in prayer. Such prayer is like a letter of acclamation to God. As it were, it calls God's attention to someone who has helped us. It asks God to bless that person specially. It asks God to reward that helper for the generosity shown to us.

Who do you need to commend to God in prayer? Perhaps it is a friend who has done something unusual for you. Perhaps it is your company for providing you employment. Perhaps it is your pastor for nourishing your soul each Sunday from God's Word. Perhaps it is your spouse for standing by you through many difficult years. Perhaps it is your children for bringing you such delight.

Whatever the reason, a prayer of commendation is a good way to show our gratitude. Whoever the person, a prayer of commendation expresses a grateful heart.

More on Boaz

Naomi's excitement probably mystified Ruth. Yes, Ruth was happy about her success. She knew that something unusual had happened in the field. She could also see that the name "Boaz" had delighted Naomi. She heard Naomi's happy prayer of gratitude for him. But she did not understand why.

Of course, we know why. In fact, we know more about Boaz than Ruth at this point. In Ruth 2:1, we learned who Boaz was. Meanwhile, Ruth had probably wondered to herself, "Who is this man, Boaz? Why did his name make Naomi so happy?"

Naomi apparently noticed Ruth's puzzled look. At the close of verse 20, she explained just who this man was. First, she told Ruth that Boaz was "our close relative." The Hebrew term *(qārôb)* literally meant "close one." Sometimes it referred to immediate family members (Lev. 21:2-3), other times to a wider circle of relatives (Ex. 32:27; 2 Sam. 19:43). So, though we learn that Boaz was a close relative of the women, we cannot be certain how close.

That still did not fully explain Naomi's joy, however. So she added, "He is one of our kinsman-redeemers" (Heb. *gō'ēl*, pronounced "go-AIL"). In Israel, the *gō'ēls* were a circle of close relatives whose duty it was to protect weak clan members (see Lev. 25).

They were to buy back land which poor relatives had mortgaged (vv. 25-30). They were also to buy the freedom of relatives whose poverty had forced them into slavery (vv. 47-55). In addition, they helped family members get justice in court (Prov. 23:11). In sum, whatever the specific need, the duty of a *gō'ēl* was to keep the family and its property together.

What did Naomi have in mind here? We cannot be certain. A *gō'ēl* was responsible for many things. So Naomi's short, vague remark makes us very curious about Boaz. We wonder whether Boaz's family ties will eventually help Naomi and Ruth. At the same time, we share some of Naomi's excitement. Boaz was family, and Israelite family members looked out for each other. He had already generously given them food.

At least they were not alone now. They had linked up with a close relative who cared. No wonder Naomi seemed more happy than bitter. And who knows what might come of this? Naomi might even yet get a son!

Gratitude in Action

At last, the widows turned their attention to the following day. Ruth briefed Naomi on what had happened earlier: "He even said to me, 'Stay with my workers until they finish harvesting all my grain' " (Ruth 2:21). Ruth was no longer just a gleaner—an outsider. She belonged with Boaz's workers. Indeed, his decree probably meant they would treat her kindly—she was a favorite of the boss.

Notice also that Ruth had permission to work the entire harvest. According to 1:22, the monthlong barley harvest had just begun. And a month of wheat harvest would follow. In Israel, those two crops made up most of the harvesttime (Joel 1:11). So the entire harvest would last about two months—from late April to early June.

This provision of Boaz is important for two reasons. First, it assured Ruth and Naomi of food for the coming year. Ruth would not waste time wandering from field to field. She would have steady work in Boaz's fields. And Boaz had guaranteed that she would have plenty of grain to gather (Ruth 2:16).

An ephah a day would feed the two widows well until the next harvest. And their diet would have variety—both barley and wheat. In short, Boaz resolved the book's first tragic theme, the lack of food. Famine had sent Naomi's family to exile in Moab. Now there was food aplenty.

Second, the provision of Boaz meant that he and Ruth might get to know each other better. The two had already talked (vv. 8-14), and Boaz knew of Ruth's fine reputation (v. 11). Presumably, during future visits by Boaz, the two could talk further. After all, they were "close" family. Who knows what might come from such talks?

Naomi, however, cautioned Ruth with some instruction of her own. She said, "It will be good for you, my daughter, to go with his girls" (v. 22). In verse 21, "workers" included both males and females. Here Naomi told Ruth to work only with Boaz's female workers. Why? Was her aim to short-circuit romances with the young men? No. Her concern was to protect Ruth—"because in someone else's field you might be harmed."

What "harm" did Naomi foresee? Elsewhere, the Hebrew word *(pāga')* commonly meant both "to meet, encounter" and "to attack violently." Neither of those meanings seems to fit here. For Ruth to meet another in a field should cause Naomi no alarm. And harvest fields were public places—unlikely places for rape or murder.

More likely, the word has a meaning similar to three other words in the chapter. In verse 9, Boaz had assured Ruth that his workers would not touch her. Later, he ordered them neither to embarrass (v. 15) nor rebuke her (v. 16). Thus, *pāga'* probably meant "to abuse." Naomi probably referred to minor verbal or physical abuse—the snide insults and rough-housing typical of young men. By working with the women, Ruth would avoid such abuse.

Now it is significant that both Boaz and Naomi sought to protect Ruth. This reminds us of her vulnerability in the field. She was a female in a society dominated by males. The young field hands could make suggestive advances, and she could do nothing but ignore them. She was also a Moabite among Israelites. Hence, the young men might ridicule Ruth's race.

Again, Ruth's only recourse was to remain silent. To reply would just inspire the young bucks to sharpen their ridicule. So, Ruth showed remarkable courage to venture into the fields. And Naomi and Boaz showed faithfulness to her by providing her protection.

Gratitude as Enjoyment

To close the scene, the narrator stepped forward with a comment: "So Ruth stayed close to the servant girls of Boaz to glean until the barley and wheat harvests were finished" (Ruth 2:23). The words are very similar to those of verse 21. They stressed that Ruth faithfully followed the instructions of Boaz and Naomi. She gleaned close to the young women.

Did Ruth bring home more ephahs of grain? Did she make

any friends among the workers? Did she and Boaz become friends? Did she suffer any harm? All the author said was that Ruth "lived with her mother-in-law" (v. 23). Verse 23, however, teaches us a third way to express gratitude: enjoy the gifts we receive.

Remember that the widows could have reacted to Boaz's generosity in several ways. Suppose they suspected hidden motives on his part. Was he using them to enhance his reputation in town? Did he expect some return on his investment—perhaps free housework by Ruth? Was he angling for Ruth to become his concubine but not his wife? Given such suspicions, the women might have rejected Boaz's offer. Ruth would have kept her distance, moving on to other fields—and probably gathered much less grain.

Or, suppose the generosity had embarrassed them. They might have felt unworthy of it. What had they done to deserve such kindness? They might have felt it wrong to take advantage of Boaz. He had been far too kind to them already. Besides, he was a relative—how could they take advantage of a relative? Or they might have worried about repaying Boaz. They were penniless—how could they ever return such a favor? Such thoughts might also have made the women reject Boaz's offer.

Instead, without hesitation, Naomi and Ruth took full advantage of Boaz's gift. Ruth did exactly what Boaz and Naomi had instructed. The widows fully enjoyed what God, through Boaz, had given them.

God has showered us with blessings. He has given us a beautiful world, beloved friends and family, caring pastors, and meaningful service for God. One way to show our gratitude is to enjoy fully what God has given us. Granted, we are unworthy of His gifts. But that unworthiness should not keep us from taking full advantage of them. After all, if God did not want us to enjoy them, He would not have given them!

Personal Gratitude

Each November 11th, I thank God for another year of life. I have a very personal reason for doing so. On that date in

Gratitude

1971, I was wounded in a mine explosion in Vietnam. I was inside a building preparing to lead worship when the mine buried in the ground outside exploded. Providentially, a refrigerator between me and the mine absorbed most of the blast. I received only minor wounds in the foot.

Now I am firmly convinced that God placed that refrigerator there for my protection. Hence, I view my life since 1971 as a precious gift from God. Each November 11th, I spend time in prayer worshiping God and expressing my deep gratitude.

But I also show my gratitude by enjoying his other gifts. My wife and I are about to celebrate twenty-two years of marriage. In 1972, our first son was born. In 1976, I started my ministry as a seminary professor. The next year, our second son was born. I have many blessings—a fine family, good friends, good health, and meaningful work. Yes, I am unworthy of them all. I cannot explain why I lived while others died. I can, however, live out my gratitude to God by enjoying God's gifts just as Ruth did.

And so can you. What generosity has God showered on you? Do you feel unworthy? Does that feeling keep you from enjoying His gifts fully? Naomi and Ruth point out three ways to show true gratitude: to praise God for His goodness, to pray for those who benefit us, and to enjoy what we have. To do so is to be truly grateful. And to be truly grateful is to show faithfulness to God in our everyday lives.

Daily, our prayer ought to be like that of English poet George Herbert: "Thou that hast given so much to me, give one thing more, a grateful heart" (*The Country Parson, The Temple*, ed. John N. Wall, Jr. [New York/Ramsey/Toronto: Paulist Press, 1981], 245).

Chapter Eight
Ingenuity: Faithfulness Seizes Opportunity
Ruth 3:1-5

Her words fell like a bombshell in the boardroom. For an icy, silent instant, the group discussion froze. The other women sat there stunned. Their puzzled stares begged the speaker for an explanation. My wife's mother, a board member, had simply said, "Ladies, we have the opportunity to answer our own prayer."

The board was that of a denominational women's missionary society. They were discussing the financial needs of a particular missionary. They had just prayed that the Lord would provide the money. Then the bomb fell. A moment later, my mother-in-law explained herself.

She recalled the treasurer's report given earlier. She pointed out that the board had a sizable balance in its account. That amount would easily meet the missionary's needs, she said. Rather than pray, she suggested that the board give the missionary the money. They immediately did! They answered their own prayer!

Is that heresy? At first glance, it seems so. The reason is that we usually assume several things about the Christian life. First, we believe that only God can solve our problems. Only heaven has the resources to help us. So, troubles turn us immediately to God. Second, we assume that only God Himself can answer prayer—and without human help. We consider it blasphemy to think that someone else could answer our prayer. And who of us would dare insult the Lord Almighty?

Finally, we treasure the idea of living by faith. Our daily creed is, "We walk by faith, not by sight" (2 Cor. 5:7). That is, avoiding trust in human institutions, abilities, or plans, we aim to live like children. In simple trust, we depend only on our loving Heavenly Father. That is what it means to please Him.

As a result, to solve an everyday problem, most of us follow a simple two-step method. The method is rooted in biblical truth. We pray about the matter. That step, as it were, puts it in God's in-basket for Him to settle. It relieves us of responsibility — we need do nothing more. It also rids us of anxiety. Obeying 1 Peter 5:7, we have cast it on Him. The worries are now His.

Next, we patiently wait for God to act. We follow the psalmist's advice, "Wait for the Lord" (Pss. 27:14; 37:34). Meanwhile, we persistently pray about the concern, as if we thought God might forget about it. Like a salesman closing a deal, we continue to press God for an answer. After all, we know that God honors persistent prayer (Luke 11:5-8; James 5:16-18).

In conclusion, simple trust and fervent prayer are the keys. For us, faith means to trust God to intervene. Along the same line, faithfulness is the patience to wait for His intervention. To do otherwise is to rely on something (or someone) other than God. That, we think, shows a lack of faith. And without faith, we might as well not be Christians at all.

Now this approach is a good one. It rests on a solid foundation of biblical truth. The Bible clearly teaches an attitude of childlike dependence on God (Matt. 6:25-34). Though true, the approach is too narrow.

First, it sees God as passive, not active. It assumes that He is not already busy executing plans of His own. It treats Him like a heavenly repairman sitting by the phone waiting for our call. On call, He only acts when we need Him.

The Bible, however, portrays God as busy pursuing His own plans in the world. After all, He reigns as King of the universe (Pss. 10:16; 47:7-8). He moves whole nations for His purposes (Amos 9:7). He appoints and deposes world leaders (Rom. 13:1). He brings their wars to an end (Ps. 46:9). The nations are His servants, not He theirs.

Further, God initiated the plan of salvation. He called Abram, Moses, David, and the prophets. He sent Jesus to be the world's Savior (John 3:16). He sent John the Baptist to announce Jesus' arrival (1:6). Only God knows the timing of Jesus' future return (Matt. 24:36; Acts 1:7).

Also, He initiated our salvation. He called us when we were hopelessly lost. If He had not drawn us first, none of us would have been saved (John 6:44; Eph. 1:4). God is not passively waiting for our initiative. Rather, God is already at work on His plans.

Second, the common view of prayer also overlooks our role in those plans. We are the ones sitting by the phone! With Moses, we bow before the burning bushes of God's guidance (Ex. 3). Like Samuel, we are to be listening for God's call to service (1 Sam. 3). Like Paul, we receive, not conceive, the Macedonian vision—God's marching orders for our next service (Acts 16:6-10; cf. 18:9).

With the disciples, we watch for the "signs of the times"—the visible proof that God is bringing history to an end (Matt. 24:42). The key word is "watch." We are to be watching for God's movements. When we see Him at work near us, that is our signal to join Him. And God desires us to apply our gifts and abilities to the task.

That is what Naomi did. We recall her earlier prayer that Ruth (and Orpah) obtain new husbands (Ruth 1:8-9). Her blessings (2:19-20) implied that she recognized God at work behind the scenes.

Apparently, she saw His hand behind Boaz's kind treatment of Ruth. In the following scene, she acts to take full advantage of an opportunity.

In so doing, she models another aspect of faithfulness: faithfulness applies human ingenuity to seize God-given opportunities. She will also show us three principles of how such faithfulness works.

Ingenuity

Opportunity's Knock

Chapter 3 presents a new Naomi. Chapter 1 pictured her as a beaten, bitter old woman. Anger against God churned inside her. Hopelessness hung heavily over her. In chapter 2, Naomi seemed passive, broken in spirit. It was Ruth who took the initiative to provide food; Naomi weakly gave approval. While Ruth worked, Naomi stayed home. She was either too weak or too depressed to assist.

Here, however, Naomi initiated things. Suddenly, she shed the shackles of passivity and took charge. Her earlier bitterness had fled. Unlike chapter 2, she instructed, her voice strong and enthusiastic, while Ruth listened. She spoke with authority and self-assurance, and an inner excitement — even joy — that something happy was about to happen. This time, Ruth would carry out Naomi's wishes (Ruth 3:5).

Naomi said, "My daughter, should I not try to find a home for you, where you will be well provided for?" (v. 1) Carefully notice her words. The word "home" (Heb. *mānôᵃḥ*) literally meant "resting place." The word is a synonym for the word "rest" (Heb. *mᵉnûḥâ*) used in Naomi's prayer (1:9). Earlier I pointed out how that word meant "place of settled security." In the Book of Ruth, both terms refer to the security and stability of marriage.

So Naomi began to play matchmaker for Ruth. More important, by punning here on the word in 1:9, Naomi gave her declaration added significance. She had prayed that God would give Ruth "rest" (i.e., a marriage). Now she stated her own intention to find Ruth "rest." In other words, Naomi was going to answer her own prayer!

Why this "born-again" Naomi? Apparently, the happy events of chapter 2 gave her a new lease on life. Boaz's kindness shook some of the hopelessness from her life. At least she and Ruth now had two blessings — food to eat and a close relative who cared (2:19-23). The two widows would not starve to death. They had plenty of grain.

They also had an ally against future uncertainties. Boaz's social stature was like money in the bank. If necessary, they could draw on it for protection. Faint rays of hope feebly pierced the oppressive, gloomy overcast of chapter 1.

More important, Naomi heard the knock of golden opportunity. In 3:2 she explained it to Ruth. The opportunity was twofold. First, Ruth had a positive relationship with Boaz, a close relative. She said, "Is not Boaz, with whose servant girls you have been, a kinsman of ours?"

Though a different word, "kinsman" built on Naomi's earlier revelation that Boaz was a kinsman-redeemer (Heb. *gō'ēl;* see 2:20). Naomi implied that he had a family obligation to consider marrying Ruth. That was the reason that Ruth should approach him rather than someone else.

Second, Naomi added, "Tonight he will be winnowing barley on the threshing floor" (v. 2). Some background on Israel's agricultural practices explains Naomi's remark. A threshing floor was a large open space of hard-packed earth or bedrock. Two phases of harvest took place there. Farmers threshed the grain—that is, beat or crushed it to remove its husk. Then they "winnowed" it—threw it into the breeze to separate the grain from the chaff. The wind would blow chaff away because it was lighter. Being heavier, the grain would fall to the floor. As we noted earlier, Bethlehem's threshing floor probably lay downhill from the city. Ruth went down to reach it (v. 6).

This was Naomi's point: tonight Boaz would be in a secluded place away from town. Darkness and distance would provide privacy for the little chat Naomi had in mind.

Naomi saw that need and opportunity had intersected. Ruth needed a husband and the situation suited making Boaz a proposal. Now Naomi did not directly credit the Lord with this bit of luck, but indirectly she did. This brings out the first principle of how faithful ingenuity works. Christians should assume that such intersections of need and opportunity come from God.

We know that God is busily at work in His world. So, as Christians we should live with an attitude of expectancy. We can presume that God's hand lies behind such opportunities—or at least desire to capitalize on them for God's glory. Thus, we show that we expect God to make opportunities for touching the lives of needy people.

I saw one example of this in 1982. That year, a friend of ours enlisted my wife's help to start a new ministry in Denver. In Oregon, Dan had met David, a disabled man who founded Tryad Ministries. David had seen a need and an opportunity—the lack of good Bible teaching for Christian disabled adults. Tryad was founded to meet this need and now sponsors annual Bible conferences at an Oregon Christian conference center. David had challenged Dan to start another Tryad Ministries in Colorado.

Dan saw both the need and the opportunity to do it. So serious preparations began for a weekend retreat. The major problem was to find enough able-bodied people to help severely disabled campers with dressing and meals. I have never forgotten what my wife said just before that weekend.

She totaled up the number of disabled and able-bodied campers registered. The camp was going to be short of able-bodied people. With quiet confidence, she said, "It will be interesting to see how God puts this one together."

That is Naomi's attitude of expectancy! That is the confidence that God is busy working His will in His world. That is the trust which believes that God enlists us in that work. That is the outlook which sees God at work when human need meets the opportunity to solve it. That is the faithfulness of the ingenious Christian.

Now the question is, Is our attitude one of expectancy? Do we expect to see God at work? Do we believe that opportunities are God-given? The "clever Christian" believes that when need and opportunity cross paths, God is at work!

The Preparations

Naomi intended to play matchmaker for Ruth and Boaz. Her scheme involved three phases, each carefully calculated to have the right effect. The first was preparation. Naomi instructed Ruth, "Wash and perfume yourself, and put on your best clothes" (Ruth 3:3). Ruth was not to rush down to Boaz right away. She still smelled sweaty from her day's work.

No, the matter was not to be hurried. Naomi wanted to

ensure that Ruth made a good impression on Boaz. So Ruth was to bathe herself—to be clean of dirt and odor. Next Ruth was to put on some perfume (Heb. lit. "to pour, anoint"). In the ancient Near East, scented oils were used for cleansing (2 Sam. 14:2; Micah 6:15). Their scents pleased ancient peoples as much as they please us today (Song 1:3). Likewise, Naomi wanted the smell of Ruth's presence to please Boaz.

Finally, Ruth was to dress smartly (Heb. lit. "put your clothes on"). Like other ancient women, Ruth would wear a tunic as an undergarment and then wrap herself in a large square mantle. Archeologists confirm that ancient peoples used colors and decorative weaving for adornment. As a poor woman, however, Ruth's wardrobe was probably very plain.

Of course, the purpose of these preparations was obvious—to make Ruth very attractive to Boaz. Her attitude was not, "Accept me just as I am, honey." She was out to entice, not repulse him. She was not to gamble away the chance of marriage by inattention to her dress and smell. Instead, Ruth was to maximize her femininity. She was to look and smell her alluring best. She wanted to please her man.

Further, the preparations may even have been intended to present Ruth as a bride. Notice how the same phrase "bathe, anoint, dress up" occurs in this ancient text, a description of bridal preparations by a goddess:

> "Inanna, at the command of her mother,
> Bathed, anointed herself with goodly oil,
> Covered her body with the noble *pala*-garment,
> Took . . . , her dowry,
> Arranged the lapis lazuli about (her) neck,
> Grasped (her) seal in her hand."[5]

Though we cannot be sure, Ruth's preparations may have been those of a bride.

The Approach
The second phase of Naomi's plan was the approach. It also aimed for a specific effect. Obviously, Ruth's first step was to

go down to the threshing floor. That was where Boaz was. But the next step sounds strange. Ruth was not to rush up to Boaz and ask, "Will you marry me?" Rather, Naomi told her, "Don't let him know you are there until he has finished eating and drinking" (Ruth 3:3).

At first glance, that move made no sense. How could the two of them talk marriage if Boaz did not even know Ruth was there? A second look, however, reveals the method in Naomi's seeming madness. "Eating and drinking" was Israel's way of saying "enjoying a meal" (see v. 7; Gen. 24:54; 2 Kings 6:23). In other words, Ruth was to wait until Boaz had his dinner.

The intended effect is obvious. The bath, perfume, and nice clothes would prepare Ruth for Boaz. This move was to prepare Boaz for Ruth. There is nothing like a good meal to soften someone up to influence! So Ruth was to wait until Boaz was in good spirits. Then he would be contented—and ready to do business.

Even then, however, Ruth was to postpone the conversation. Naomi ordered, "When he lies down, note the place where he is lying. Then go and uncover his feet and lie down" (Ruth 3:4). Ruth was to conceal her presence from Boaz. From her hiding place, she was to watch where he lay down to sleep.

This step was probably more important than it sounds. The farmers of Bethlehem shared the same threshing floor. Some of them might also have spent the night there. How embarrassing for Ruth if she approached the wrong man!

Finally, she was to quietly tiptoe there, uncover his feet, and lie down to sleep. What does the "uncover-his-feet" gesture mean? Probably it was a symbolic proposal of marriage. That explanation fits well with Ruth's actual request for marriage in verse 9. In Israel, the word "feet" was a euphemism for human sexual organs (Ex. 4:25; Ezek. 16:25 [NIV has "body" for Heb. "feet:"]). Perhaps by uncovering his feet, Ruth showed her readiness for marriage (and sexual relations).

The gesture may have also served another purpose. It

probably delayed their talk until the middle of the night. Boaz would likely awaken in the middle of the night, when the chilly night air on his exposed feet would make it hard to sleep. By then, other workers would have already fallen asleep or gone home. The pair would either be alone or the only ones awake.

The final phase of the plan was to await further instructions. According to Naomi, the next move was up to Boaz: "He will tell you what to do" (Ruth 3:4). Once Ruth carried out Naomi's instructions, Boaz would reply with some instructions of his own. We are left to wonder what those might be. The answer emerges in the next scene (vv. 6-15).

Now two things about Naomi's scheme are striking. First, it seems geared to maintain secrecy. Boaz and Ruth would meet in a secluded spot at night. Ruth was to sneak up on a sleeping Boaz. They would talk in the wee hours of morning. They might even be alone. Why these precautions?

Perhaps Naomi wanted to protect both parties from embarrassment. Only they would know what took place—a happy agreement, a polite refusal, an angry rejection. The talk would not adversely influence future suitors. It might also spare both great shame. In Israel, threshing floors were the ancient "red light district," the place where prostitutes did business (Hosea 9:1). The secrecy may have headed off mistaken gossip about possible immorality.

The scheme's second striking impression is this: nothing was left to chance. The preparations—bath, perfume, and nice clothes—aimed to increase the odds of success in Ruth's favor. The approach sought to put Boaz in a good mood and free him from social pressure. In sum, the plan sought to make him open to Ruth's desire for marriage.

A Persian proverb says, "Trust God, but tie your camel." There is great biblical truth in that. Christians must trust God—but also take responsible steps to do God's will. That is just the balance which Naomi's plan sought to strike. Naomi could not determine how Boaz would react to Ruth's visit. It might honor, horrify, or anger him. But she could—and did—control as many things as possible.

She did not "wait on the Lord" to intervene—she got to work. She applied her human ingenuity to the situation. She joined responsible, creative human efforts with a firm trust in God's blessing. She assumed that God's work was a cooperative venture between her and God.

God still functions that way. He leads the way by being at work in the world. His work gives us opportunities to serve Him. We respond to His initiative by applying our human ingenuity to take advantage of the opportunity. This brings out the second principle of ingenuity. Faithfulness means doing everything humanly possible with an opportunity and leaving the outcome to God.

My wife Pam and our friend Dan followed this principle. The first Colorado Tryad retreat came from careful planning and hard work. Their approach was not passive but active. They did not simply pray, "O Lord, please provide a spiritual retreat for Colorado's disabled." They did pray—fervently in fact—for God's guidance and blessing.

But they also applied their human abilities—creativity, persistence, and compassion—to the opportunity. They formed a steering committee, held planning meetings, made contacts, spread publicity, and raised money. And God blessed their efforts with a good turnout and genuine spiritual impact. Years later, the ministry continues.

That is ingenuity—an expression of biblical faithfulness.

The One in the Middle
For all its ingenuity, Naomi's plan assumed something— Ruth's willingness to carry it out. She, not Naomi, would run the errand to the threshing floor. She, not Naomi, would carefully uncover Boaz's feet and lie down. She, not Naomi, would suffer—or savor—his response to the symbolic gesture. Would Ruth do it?

Understand how uncomfortable this role was. Yes, Boaz had already treated her kindly. But that was an entirely different situation. In the field, they talked in public during daylight. Naomi's scheme, however, had the two talking in private in the dead of night. The risks were great.

Boaz might react wrongly to the proposal. Put yourself in his sandals for a moment. He was a highly respected civic leader in Bethlehem (Ruth 2:1). No doubt he valued his reputation. Suddenly, without warning, he finds himself sleeping with a beautiful woman!

He might explode over Naomi's little midnight surprise. He might blame Ruth for endangering his reputation. He might be offended at the very suggestion that he marry a Moabitess. Such responses could devastate poor Ruth.

Also, rumors about their meeting might circulate. Suppose someone spotted them lying together. Whispered gossip could spread through Bethlehem like wildfire. The town might brand them immoral. Legal penalties might follow. Even if no punishment fell, such slander would ruin both their reputations. And all over one single night!

One could understand if Ruth declined to play along. She probably had the most to lose. She had cut her ties with Moab. Bethlehem was now her home—and she had many years yet to live there. But now the town might throw her out as "trash." Or, if she stayed, she might always live under a cloud of moral suspicion.

Despite the risks, Ruth replied, "I will do whatever you say" (3:5). Naomi need not devise a "Plan B." Ruth agreed to obey. Notice how short Ruth's answer was. There was no hesitation or holding back. There were no conditions. She was quietly firm and resolute: "Naomi, I'll do it."

This points to the third principle of ingenuity in the service of faithfulness. Ingenuity is the willingness to do the best we can. That is what pleases God. God does not expect perfection. He does not even expect "success," at least not success measured by human standards. He simply wants a willingness to serve. He desires only that we do the best we can. That is what Ruth agreed to do—to do her best with Naomi's plan. That is all God expects of us.

The Expectant Life

No one would have predicted what a young Christian, Laurence C. Jones, accomplished. But his story illustrates what this chapter is about.[6] Jones lived in the late 1800s in Saint Joseph, Missouri. His father was a hotel porter, so his family was poor. Back then, prejudice and poverty prevented poor black children from finishing school or going to college. Through ingenuity and hard work, however, Jones graduated from Iowa State University.

In college, the great black educator, Booker T. Washington, became his inspiration. Jones saw the need for better education among poor, Southern blacks. After graduation, Jones set out to teach among them in Hinds County, Mississippi. One Christmas, he visited needy families in the Piney Woods area. The visit showed him that here was his opportunity. He decided to found his own school there.

In 1907, with $1.65 in cash, he started the Piney Woods Country Life School. Jones taught three pupils around a pine stump classroom. Over the years, normal classrooms replaced the stump and new teachers joined his forces. Today, the student body of Piney Woods numbers more than 400. Hundreds of its graduates have learned practical trades there. Many others have gone on to graduate from college.

Looking back, Jones realized that God's guidance lay behind his endeavor. He saw God's hand behind his decision to go South. He knew God had heard the cries of black people in Piney Woods for better education. Jones knew that God had sent him to meet the need denied God's people.

Jones had a simple formula for success: "Keep on praying as if everything depends on God, and keep on working as if everything depends on you. You cannot get discouraged if you do that." That formula captures the proper balance between human ingenuity and trust in God. Faithfulness is to do both—to take advantage of opportunities as given by God and to pray for God's blessing.

Now the question is, what need have you been praying about lately? Do you have the opportunity—the ability, the means—to answer your own prayer? Do you sense God's providence behind that opportunity? If so, what common ingenuity, what simple plan, might touch that need in Jesus' name? As Naomi showed, Christian faithfulness is to apply our human ingenuity to seize such opportunities. We assume they come from God.

As you, like Naomi, ponder your opportunity and your plan, make this your prayer:

No service in itself is small;
None great, though earth it fill.
But that is small that seeks its own,
And great that seeks God's will.

Then hold my hand, most gracious Lord,
Guide all my goings still;
And let it be my life's one aim
To know and do Thy will.

      (Author unknown)

Chapter Nine
Self-Sacrifice: Faithfulness Honors Others
Ruth 3:6-11

According to a friend of mine, the world has two kinds of people. Most people are of the "Here-I-am" type. Such people always want to call attention to themselves, to have other people notice them. In groups, they dress and behave to attract attention. They brag about their latest achievements.

In conversation, "Here-I-am" people always talk about what interests them—their jobs, their children, their vacations, their favorites. Even when others speak, they insist on giving their opinion and setting others straight. At work, they always maneuver for recognition by the boss. They sit next to him at lunch, mimic his ideas, and strive to impress him.

The other basic type of people are the "There-you-are" people. These people love to call attention to other people, especially those often overlooked. In groups, they enjoy introducing shy people to their friends and making them feel comfortable. They good-naturedly brag about the achievements of others.

In conversation, they love listening to what is happening to others—their jobs, their children, their vacations, their favorites. They would rather draw out the thoughts of others than narrate their own. At work, they work steadily behind the scenes letting the boss notice others. They let others sit next to him at lunch, take seriously his ideas, and praise the job he is doing.

103

Sadly, the world tends to honor the "Here-I-am" type. It loves the person of "ambition" and "drive." It admires someone "who lets nothing stop him" and "who never takes 'no' for an answer." It cheers the one who takes charge and shouts, "I'm the greatest!" It rewards those whose theme song is "I Did It My Way."

By contrast, the Bible honors self-sacrifice, not self-centeredness. It praises the "There-you-are" type of person. Such a person invests herself in others and gives himself to others. She sacrifices her own interests for the interests of others. He sets aside his own desires to help others reach theirs. Such people pattern their lifestyle after Jesus, the One who sacrificed His own life to save the world.

Ruth was such a person. We have already seen her great devotion to Naomi. In the scene which follows, she will even top that deed. We will witness an unexpected, remarkable act of self-sacrifice as we watch Ruth and Boaz teach us three things about another aspect of faithfulness—self-sacrifice.

The Scene

Ruth now carried out Naomi's plan. She "went down to the threshing floor and did everything her mother-in-law told her to do" (Ruth 3:6). Now imagine the scene. Night had fallen on Bethlehem. The streets were dark except for the candle-glow seeping out under doorways. Only occasional, muffled bursts of laughter disturbed the quiet.

Outside the city, a hushed chill hovered in the air. Like distant, feeble fires overhead, stars fought futilely against the growing gloom. Normal sights—the nearby harvest fields, roads stretching in the distance, the faraway mountains of Moab—lurked invisibly in the darkness. A deathly silence gripped the landscape. Only the rhythmic protests of crickets eluded its grasp. The terrain seemed desert-like—dark, silent, uninhabited.

Into the murky gloom waded Ruth on her secret mission. Silently she crept down the street, peeked around the corner, and headed for the city gate. The only sound was the racket of her pounding heart. She prayed no one would hear it!

Quietly she slipped undetected from the sleeping city. Fortunately, unexpected allies joined her cause. Surrounding shadows camouflaged her movements. Cricket cries covered the scratch of her footsteps on the path. Quickly she put distance between herself and the town.

Farther down the path, her inner panic subsided, her pace relaxed. Steadily she walked toward her goal. Occasionally, hearing suspicious sounds, she hid in a pool of darkness until certain she was alone. On she went. Twenty minutes later, she picked out the shadowy contours of the threshing floor just ahead.

Now her heartbeat grew louder and panic returned. "Here at last," she whispered softly to herself. She slowed her pace, fixing her gaze squarely on her target. Hurriedly, her mind reviewed Naomi's instructions again: "Do not let him know you are there."

As if stalking game, she stealthily crept to the edge of the threshing floor. There she stopped, frozen as a statue, hidden in the shadows. From her secret post, she silently surveyed the scene. The air was chilly, hushed, and heavy with the smell of fresh grain. Its sweet scent almost soothed her fears. Dimly she made out various piles of grain.

Finally, she spotted him—Boaz—barely visible in the starlight, enjoying his supper. She smiled to herself, a little relieved. "At least I will not uncover the wrong set of feet," she thought. Now she wondered, "Has he noticed me?" Apparently not. She breathed a sigh of relief. Then, as if taking aim, her eyes locked on Boaz as he went about his business.

The Approach

As she watched, Boaz finished his dinner (Ruth 3:7). The food and drink left Boaz "in good spirits." So far, Naomi's strategy seemed to be working. Boaz was in a good mood—and vulnerable to influence!

Apparently, the dinner also made Boaz drowsy. He went "to lie down at the far end of the grain pile." Offstage, Ruth remembered Naomi's words, "When he lies down, note the place where he is lying." Obediently, Ruth tracked his movement across the threshing floor. She carefully noted the exact spot where he lay.

Why did he make his bed beside the grain pile? Some think he was there to protect his grain against thieves. Others suggest that he was there to celebrate some kind of ceremony, maybe even a religious one. Or perhaps, like the modern executive who sleeps in his office, he simply wanted to get an early start on tomorrow's work. We cannot be certain. In any case, sleepy but contented, Boaz stretched out on the floor.

Again, a little imagination brings this scene to life. The mood of Boaz was mellow, relaxed. Perhaps he surveyed the starry splendor splashed across the sky. He sniffed the sweet smell of success—the scent of abundant, fresh grain beside him. Perhaps his mind spun aimlessly through various subjects—tomorrow's schedule, calculations of profits, pilgrimages to the temple, future plans.

He felt a warm sense of well-being. He was the very portrait of someone enjoying "the good life." He never suspected that a woman lurked offstage in the darkness. He would find out soon enough! Finally, at some point, he dropped peacefully off to sleep.

Nearby, Ruth probably could not see Boaz doze off. She watched and waited. Perhaps she sensed signs of sleep—deep breathing, a lack of movement, even light snoring. When she was certain of his slumber, she softly tiptoed from the shadows across to him. Following Naomi's orders, she uncovered his feet and lay down.

At first, I imagine she lay stiff as a corpse waiting for Boaz to awaken. Her muscles tensed, her heart pounded wildly, her ears listened for movement. Beads of sweat moistened her brow. She worried about her perfume hiding the odor. She prayed for God's help. Perhaps she suddenly felt strange lying with a man—stranger than being a Moabite in Israel.

Minutes passed and nothing happened. The crisis past, she relaxed her vigil. "So far so good. Boaz, have I got a surprise for you!" She laughed to herself in relief. Settling more comfortably, perhaps her eyes scanned the distant starry sky. Its shining splendor eased her fears.

More minutes passed. Gradually, drowsiness overtook her and she, like Boaz, drifted off to sleep. Unlike Boaz, however, she was too keyed up for sound sleep. She probably dozed fitfully, fear fighting drowsiness for attention.

Now freeze that mental frame for a moment: a prominent civic leader and an alien woman sleeping together. Stuff for a scandal, for sure! What the gossips of Bethlehem would make of that!

At the same time, that picture reminds us of Ruth's courage. She put her reputation on the line to execute Naomi's plan. The risk of public shame cruelly stalked her steps, but she never wavered from her goal. Her promise to Naomi was more important than what other people might think of her.

Throughout the Bible, God's servants always put promises before popularity. Consider how poor Daniel suffered. He had won a full scholarship to King's College, the University of Babylon. After graduation, he had a guaranteed cushy job with the government (Dan. 1:3-5, 18-21). His brilliance soon impressed two kings (Dan. 2; 5). He was on a fast track to the top! (2:48; 5:29) In fact, he was just about to get the ultimate promotion (6:3).

The government, however, enacted a law which, on penalty of death, required everyone to pray only to the king (6:7-9). Daniel refused. He was willing to spoil the king's good impression of him. He was ready to lose that prestigious promotion. He had promised to pray to God alone, however unpopular that might be with the king (v. 10).

Consider the case of Jesus. His own home church had kicked Him out for heresy (Luke 4:16-30). What a reputation He had: "Here is a glutton and a drunkard, a friend of tax collectors and 'sinners' " (7:34).

One day, after Jesus preached, a pastor invited Him home to dinner (vv. 36-50). A local prostitute began to bathe and perfume His feet.

Jesus faced a choice—receive the woman's kindness or push her away. The temptation was to reject her in order to please His "holy" host. Here was a golden opportunity for the itinerant preacher from Galilee. He could score some points with the local clergy by throwing her out. Here was the chance to redeem His reputation—to end all suspicions about His righteousness. He might even get more speaking engagements in synagogues!

Instead, Jesus chose compassion over contempt. Why? Because His mission was to give such sinners forgiveness. He would not swerve from that purpose. He did not care what others thought about Him. He only cared what pleased God.

That is the first thing Ruth teaches us about self-sacrifice. Self-sacrifice may require risking our reputations to do what pleases God. It means doing what God wants regardless of what others think. This is the self-sacrifice which God desires faithful Christians to show.

Ruth's Surprise

Ruth and Boaz probably lay together for several hours. Boaz slept peacefully unaware of her presence. Ruth rested as well as she could. Then, in the middle of the night, something happened (Ruth 3:8). Sadly, the details are unclear because the first two Hebrew words are unclear. The NIV says "startled" since elsewhere the first word (*ḥārad*) means "to tremble with fear" (Ex. 19:16; 1 Sam. 14:15).

On the other hand, *ḥārad* can mean simply "tremble" without fear as a cause (Gen. 27:33; Ex. 19:18). The author said nothing about Boaz being afraid. He did not even know Ruth was there. So, I would render the word "trembled." That is, Boaz "shivered" from the chilly air on his exposed feet.

The second word (*lāpat*) is even harder to define than *ḥārad*. This word is used only one other time in the Bible, and that's in Job 6:18, itself a difficult verse. Related words in Arabic, however, suggest that *lāpat* probably meant "to turn (oneself) over" or "to feel, grope." If so, Boaz either "groped" for a way to cover his feet or "rolled over," perhaps to get more comfortable. Whatever his movements, they produced a surprising discovery—a woman was lying at his feet!

Now, surprises strike people differently. They terrify some people. (They are the people who always avoid haunted houses on Halloween.) "Don't scare me like that!" such folks reply. Surprises anger other people. "Don't you ever do that to me again!" they exhort the jokesters. These folks are worriers, people nervously striving to keep life under control. Surprises threaten that control.

Others find surprises exciting. "Wow, that was great—scary but great!" they exult. They are the ones who love carnival rides and roller coasters! Still others are impossible to surprise. They are so suspicious that they notice everything. They are always on guard against conspiracies by friends. So, no one ever throws them a surprise party! The question here was, how would Boaz react—angry, pleased, offended, embarrassed? And would he tell Ruth what was to happen next as Naomi had said? (Ruth 3:4)

Probably a tense, silent instant passed. The two simply stared at each other, Boaz in shock, Ruth in fear. Then Boaz reacted with a question: "Who are you?" (v. 9) In Hebrew, "you" is feminine singular. That shows that Boaz knew the figure lying in the shadows was a woman. Perhaps the perfume, dress style, or hair length gave away Ruth's gender. But Boaz wanted to know the identity of this mysterious woman with whom he was dealing.

Ruth quickly answered, "I am your servant Ruth." Though unimportant at first glance, this simple exchange revealed much. For the first time, Ruth identified herself by name. She was no longer just Naomi's daughter-in-law or the Moabite gleaner Boaz had met in his field. She was now a person in her own right. She spoke to him as a near equal—as Ruth to Boaz.

Further, the exchange signaled that Ruth was no longer just a poor Moabite immigrant. Contrast this scene with what happened in Ruth 2. There, Boaz spoke about her to his foreman, but he did not speak to her directly at first. And he did not ask who she was but who owned her ("Whose is she?" v. 5).

Ruth 2 called Ruth "the Moabitess" (vv. 2, 21; cf. 1:22; 2:6). That implied that she was still a foreigner living on foreign soil. Fittingly, Ruth bowed humbly before Boaz as if unworthy of his notice (v. 10). Chapter 3, by contrast, completely dropped the term "Moabitess." It portrayed her as a good match for a leading Bethlehemite citizen like Boaz.

Finally, in Ruth 2, Ruth called herself a "maidservant" (*shiphâ*, v. 13, NASB), a term usually reserved for servant-class women (Ex. 11:5; 2 Sam. 17:17). In Ruth 3, however, Ruth called herself a "servant" (*'āmâ*). This term was used for workers with close, almost family, ties to their employers (Gen. 21:10; Deut. 5:14; 16:11). Here it may even have hinted at Ruth's availability for marriage.

In summary, between chapters 2 and 3, Ruth has become more a part of Israel than before. She has a higher social status. She is no longer just "the Moabitess"—an outsider in Bethlehem. Now she is "your servant Ruth"—a person in her own right, a "household servant" worthy of marriage to a Bethlehemite.

The Proposal

After identifying herself, Ruth got down to business. She told Boaz, "Spread the corner of your garment over me, since you are a kinsman-redeemer" (Ruth 3:9). The phrase (lit.) "spread your garment-edge" meant "to marry" (Ezek. 16:8; cf. Deut. 22:30; Mal. 2:16). An ancient marriage custom probably lay behind it, a custom similar to one common among modern Arabs. To symbolize his marriage, an Arab man will throw a corner of his long garment over his new wife. So, Ruth asked Boaz to marry her.

Notice three things about Ruth's proposal. First, Ruth gave the reason that Boaz should marry her—"since you are a kinsman-redeemer." In chapter 7, I pointed out that a kinsman-redeemer (*gō'ēl*) was a close relative responsible for aiding needy family members. For example, he would buy back property which a poor relative had mortgaged to get some money (Lev. 25:25). Remember also that Naomi had told Ruth that Boaz was a *gō'ēl*.

Why should Boaz marry Ruth because he was a kinsman-redeemer? Because kinsman-redeemers had an additional duty—to marry the widows of dead relatives who had no children. Their marriage was to produce a child to carry on the family line. In this case, if the *gō'ēl* Boaz married Ruth, Israel would consider their firstborn child to be Naomi's legal heir (see Ruth 4:5, 10). That child would keep Naomi's family from dying out.

Notice a second thing. Apparently, Ruth was to be a substitute for Naomi in this transaction. Recall that Naomi was the widow of Elimelech—Ruth was merely her daughter-in-law. So, according to custom, Boaz should have married Naomi, not Ruth. The problem, however, was that Naomi was physically unable to have children.

Evidently, Israelite practice allowed another relative—in this case, Ruth—to substitute for such a widow. That made sense because Ruth was the widow of Naomi's late son. She was also Naomi's closest friend. In sum, this marriage was for more than love. It aimed to keep Naomi's family alive.

Third, in proposing Ruth used a key word from Ruth 2. The word "garment-edge" is the Hebrew word *kānāp*. In verse 12, Boaz used the same word in the sense of "wings." He had prayed that the God under whose "wings" Ruth had sought refuge would repay her devotion. In 3:9, Ruth used *kānāp*, asking Boaz to spread his wing—that is, garment-edge—over her. In other words, Ruth applied to Boaz himself something he had said to her.

Ruth was asking Boaz to answer his own prayer. He had prayed that God, her protector, would reward her. Here, she asked him to be her protector through marriage. In modern terms, she subtly said, "Boaz, put your money where your mouth is. Here's your chance to provide me refuge as part of God's reward. Your 'garment-edge' (*kānāp*) will be God's 'wings' (*kānāp*) of refuge for me."

Now came the moment of truth. How would Boaz react? Would it be wedding bells or wailing walls for Ruth? Fortunately, his response was positive. He praised Ruth's action: "The Lord bless you, my daughter. This kindness is greater than that which you showed earlier" (v. 10).

Earlier, Boaz had lauded Ruth's loyalty to Naomi. He praised her great sacrifice in leaving Moab, her family, and her roots. Now she had done another act of "kindness" (Heb.

ḥesed). As Ruth lay humbly at his feet, he mentally compared the two deeds side by side. "This time you've outdone even yourself!" he said.

Today people choose mates for many reasons. Some marry for love. They follow that old proverbial expression: "Love is blind and marriage an institution for the blind." They overlook—and sometimes miss!—their partner's faults. Others marry for lust. Their one desire is to satisfy their sexual passions. Glands, not the heart, dictate their choice.

Others marry for money. They may mouth "I love you for who you are," but they really only have eyes for the bank account. Their partner is a ladder to a better lifestyle. Others marry for status. When they say "I love you for who you are," they mean it—literally! For them, marriage to someone important is a stairway to higher status.

What struck Boaz was that Ruth had done none of the above. He said, "You have not run after the younger men, whether rich or poor" (v. 10). She could have courted the richest man in town or fallen for the poorest one. Instead, she chose to marry for duty. She chose a marriage that would benefit Naomi.

How strange that sounds to modern ears! We are so used to making our own plans, to living our own lives, to fulfilling our own dreams. Suppose Ruth had been a "Here-I-am" person. She would have picked a husband to meet her needs. She would have married someone to give her fulfillment. She would have wed to satisfy her own wants.

But Ruth put Naomi's needs ahead of her own. She volunteered to carry out Naomi's plan—to marry a *gō'ēl* so Naomi's family might have a child. She was a "There-you-are" person. And she teaches us a second truth about self-sacrifice: in self-sacrifice, we make it our aim to meet the needs of others, disregarding our own.

In 1961, John F. Kennedy became President of the United States. His inaugural address gave his audience a powerful challenge: "Ask not what your country can do for you, but ask what you can do for your country." Kennedy put his finger on the heart of what self-sacrifice is. It is not to ask what we can do for ourselves but what we can do for others.

Jesus taught His disciples the same truth (Matt. 20:20-28). One day, several had lobbied Jesus for key cabinet posts in His future administration. The others became jealous. But Jesus set them all straight. He reminded them of the harsh, proud Gentile rulers they knew. Then He said something shocking: "Whoever wants to become great among you must be your servant" (v. 26).

To be great is to be a humble servant, said Jesus. True greatness lies at the bottom, not the top, of the social ladder. As an example, Jesus cited Himself—"just as the Son of Man did not come to be served, but to serve, and to give His life as a ransom for many" (v. 28). No one waited on Jesus. Instead, He waited on the world. He served up His own life to save it.

My friend Margaret, a victim of multiple sclerosis, follows Jesus' model. Because of M.S., she walks slowly and with an unsteady sway. She also speaks slowly, and her voice sounds like she has a cold. Given her physical suffering, one might expect her to be a "Here-I-am" person. She has every right to stay home and receive care. She has plenty of her own needs to worry about.

As a Christian, however, she took Jesus' example of self-sacrifice seriously. She knew that many disabled adults lived in a certain downtown apartment building. She also knew how lonely, isolated, and rejected they felt. So she began to visit the building one evening each week. She would sit in the lounge and befriend anyone who happened by. Her warm, disarming smile won her many friends. Her compassion eased their many personal sorrows.

Later, she started a weekly Bible study there. She enlisted others from her church to help. Together they led a small weekly Bible study group with her new friends. Margaret could have tended to her own needs. Like Jesus and Ruth, however, she put concern for others ahead of concern for herself. She is another ordinary Christian living out biblical faithfulness today.

What about you? Do your own needs preoccupy you? Are

you ignoring needs around you? Like Margaret, you might have some good excuses for not obeying Him. You could appeal to having a lousy marriage, busy work schedule, or heavy family duties. But are you willing to follow Jesus' example? If so, look closely at people around you. See their needs. And ask God to use you to meet one of them.

Great Honor

The annual Academy Awards ceremony is always an exciting event. The gold Oscar honors the movie industry's best achievements that year. Academy members covet Oscars because they represent recognition, not by fans, but by peers—people who know what excellence in the profession is. Whatever the winner's job—actor, director, writer, designer, artist, musician—it says, "This year, you were the best."

In Ruth 3:11, Boaz honored Ruth for her Oscar-type performance. First, he eased Ruth's fears: "And now, my daughter, don't be afraid" (v. 11). Ruth need not worry about Boaz's reaction. He was not angry but compassionate. Apparently, he was prepared to treat her again with the same kindness he showed her in the field. At the words "don't be afraid," Ruth probably breathed a sigh of relief. She would come out of this mission alive!

Also, Ruth need not worry about her future. Boaz accepted Ruth's proposal: "I will do for you all you ask." For Ruth, those words were great news. "Mission accomplished!" she perhaps thought to herself. She would soon have the husband she sought. Of course, we cheer this news too. We had hoped Ruth and Boaz would marry. Now we can bring out the champagne. Our imagination starts to plan the wedding!

Finally, Boaz handed Ruth an Oscar of high praise. He said, "All my fellow townsmen know that you are a woman of noble character" (v. 11). In Hebrew, "woman of noble character" literally meant "woman of strength" ('eshet ḥayil). Elsewhere, the phrase occurs only in the Bible's portrait of the ideal wife (Prov. 12:4; 31:10). "Strength" did not refer to the woman's physical strength but her strength of character—her devotion, creativity, generosity, and industry.

114

That honor certainly fit Ruth. Bethlehem rightly saw all those commendable qualities in Ruth. She would, indeed, make someone an ideal wife. More important, however, the phrase "woman of strength" closely resembled the description of Boaz in Ruth 2:1. He was a "man of standing"—an *'ish gibbôr ḥayil* or "mighty man of strength."

This was significant. By using similar phrases for Boaz and Ruth, the Bible implied that they were a good match. That was why Boaz agreed to Ruth's wish—the whole town knew Ruth was a quality woman. They were no longer "man of standing" and "Moabitess." They were both people of high, noble character. They would make a fine couple. Here we learn a third truth about self-sacrifice.

Remember the great risks Ruth took in carrying out her mission. Remember the great self-sacrifice—her willingness to let her marriage benefit Naomi, not herself. Here Boaz praised her highly and accepted her proposal. His acceptance meant that she would now have a husband. His praise also meant that Bethlehem had accepted her too. What Boaz had prayed (v. 12), was coming true, at least in part. Boaz was answering his own prayer.

Ruth's devotion had finally paid some rewards. Through Boaz, God had paid some of her "wages." This is the truth of which she reminds us: God rewards self-sacrifice.

Throughout the Bible, God has passed out many similar "Academy Awards" for self-sacrifice. Step to the top of Mt. Moriah for such an Oscar presentation (Gen. 22). Watch Abraham draw the knife toward Isaac, his only son, as God had commanded. Hear God's urgent, "Stop, Abraham!" Listen to His word of approval, "Now I know that you fear God" (v. 12). Hear God's award citation: "I will surely bless you and make your descendants as numerous as the stars in the sky and as the sand on the seashore" (v. 17).

Step to the temple for another presentation (Luke 21:1-4). Watch the wealthy dropping big bucks in the offering plate. See the silent crowd smile its admiration. Watch the poor widow drop in two pennies. Hear their mournful "clink, clink." See the crowd whisper its disdain. But watch Jesus pass out the Oscar: "I tell you the truth ... this poor widow has put in more than all the others" (v. 3).

Finally, step to the glittering, heavenly throne room (Rev. 4–5). See the crowd bow in homage before the Great King. See them lay their crowns before His royal feet (4:10-11). Watch the King evaluate the performance of His only Son, the slain Lamb. Hear the crowd sing His award:

Worthy is the Lamb, who was slain,
   to receive power and wealth
   and wisdom and strength
and honor and glory and praise! (5:12)

God, indeed, gives His Oscars for self-sacrifice like Ruth's. All performances by His "There-you-are" people please Him a great deal. He deems such performances worthy of His recognition.

Conclusion
In his famous "Letter from a Birmingham Jail," Dr. Martin Luther King, Jr. wrote:

If today's church does not recapture the sacrificial spirit of the early church, it will lose its authenticity, forfeit the loyalty of millions, and be dismissed as an irrelevant social club with no meaning for the twentieth century (quoted from Stephen B. Oates, *Let the Trumpet Sound* [New York: Mentor Books, 1982], 221).

Those are powerful words. They warn us of a danger threatening Christians today. Modern culture promotes self-centeredness. Its ideal is the "Here-I-am" person.

But we must cultivate the opposite trait—good, old-fashioned self-sacrifice. We must please God no matter what others think. We must attend to the needs of others before satisfying our own. Only that is faithfulness to our Lord. Only then will the world truly see the God we serve. At the same time, we rest assured that God rewards our efforts.

Chapter Ten

Patience: Faithfulness Awaits the Outcome

Ruth 3:12-18

It was our annual family vacation. With excitement, we loaded up the car and headed west toward California. Dear relatives, sunny beaches, and Disneyland awaited us. But my wife was a wise, experienced parent. She knew about the mysterious boredom monster, the invisible creature which attacks small children traveling great distances by car.

Carefully, she had prepared to defeat the fiend. She had brought along all kinds of amusements for our two small boys. So, as the car hummed along the interstate, we chatted calmly. In the backseat, the boys played happily. An hour into the trip, however, our youngest suddenly leaned forward to ask, "Daddy, are we there yet?" A victory for the boredom monster!

It is hard to wait when we want to get somewhere. It is hard to wait when we want something done When it comes to patience, we are all like children cooped up in a car. Patience comes hard for all of us.

Part of the problem is cultural conditioning. We are used to instant everything. Instant coffee spares us the wait to brew it. Bank machines offer us instant cash without waiting in line or waiting for the bank to open. Businesses give us instant credit without our waiting for a credit check. Supermarkets have special checkout lines for customers buying only a few items. No need to wait long to get on with our lives.

We are simply not used to waiting for things. In fact, to wait for anything is a personal insult. It is simply un-American.

This brings up a second aspect of cultural conditioning. We have an inflated sense of self-importance. Our culture has conditioned us to think that the consumer is king. "The customer is always right—even when he's wrong," goes the popular maxim. Whatever our annual income or social status, we own the shopping mall. Store clerks treat us as if we were the King of Saudi Arabia!

Businesses curry our favor, baby our needs, and pamper our wishes. And it is not just because they like us. As a matter of fact, they do not even really *know* us! Rather, they follow a simple rule of modern business: companies which serve the customer, prosper; those which do not, fail. In short, we hold them hostage to their own profit motive.

Besides cultural conditioning, something else drives us. We know how short life is. We feel like a child who has won a shopping spree—five minutes in a toy store to collect whatever he wants. We have so many things to do yet so little time to do them. We want to be good in everything—as employees, church members, and family members. We have jobs to do, children to raise, aging parents to aid, neighbors to love, churches to serve.

Read our weekly calendar: every space is filled! We are always on the way somewhere else. Everything—meals, sleep, work, play—becomes a rush job, something to get done so we can move on to something else. We are trying to cram two (or even three!) lifetimes into one. That makes patience all the more difficult for us.

But one more thing should be said. Our impatience comes from two spiritual problems—a swollen pride and a lack of faith. The pride comes from the self-importance which the world teaches us. Because salesclerks indulge our whims, we expect life to treat us the same way.

So we swagger along expecting life, like Egypt's swirling Red Sea, somehow to part before our eyes. When the dry land fails to appear, we lose our patience. We angrily stomp along the shore fuming, "This can't happen to me!" Why not? Because pride has convinced us of our importance. Pride has dethroned patience in our heart.

A lack of faith follows this. Self-importance gives birth to blind self-confidence. We feel like spiritual Rambos who can beat back any assault life throws at us. In the process, we forget the crucial things. We forget to trust God's power to meet our needs. When a few skirmishes send us reeling, we lose our patience. Instead of calling for God's help, we redouble our efforts—only to be knocked down again.

Further, we forget to trust God's timing. When something does not happen when we want it to, we lose patience. After all, according to the Bible, God has both the power and the desire to act. Why, we ask, is He so slow in getting things done?

Someone has said, "Patience is letting your motor idle when you feel like stripping the gears." How true! And how tough to do! Our culture revs up our motors to screech into action. Like sand in an hourglass, our lifespan vanishes all too quickly. We want to pop the clutch and get moving.

But the Bible urges us toward patience. Sometimes it tells us to put life into neutral and let the motor idle. Fortunately, it offers us Ruth as an example of how to do that. As we watch the next scene, we will learn three biblical bases for patience.

Oops! A Complication

It had been quite a night for Ruth and Boaz. Her nighttime visit had taken him totally by surprise. Success followed surprise, however. Boaz agreed to Ruth's marriage proposal. He affirmed that Ruth was a good match for him. As readers, we were delighted. But suddenly, Boaz burst our bubble. He sprang a little surprise of his own.

He told Ruth, "Although it is true that I am near of kin, there is a kinsman-redeemer nearer than I" (Ruth 3:12). Surprise! Just when we thought things were all settled, Boaz threw a wrench in the works! Boaz knew that there was another, closer relative. Because he was closer, custom required that he have the first opportunity to serve as *gō'ēl*.

A bit of background will clarify this. Remember that every family had not just one kinsman-redeemer but a small group of them. Naomi had told Ruth that Boaz was one of them (see 2:20). The Bible never provides a list of kinsman-redeemers by rank, but Leviticus 25:49 lists uncles, cousins, and "any blood relative" as likely candidates for a *gō'ēl*.

Whatever the order, the point was that someone else had the right to marry Ruth first. Boaz could not violate that right. This new wrinkle requires us to look again at his acceptance of Ruth's proposal (Ruth 3:11). Evidently, when he agreed to do what she asked, Boaz simply promised to arrange a marriage. We assumed that he would be the groom. He meant that the lucky man would be either himself or the closer relative.

That is just the way life is sometimes. About the time we near the finish line, somebody moves it! No sooner have we pumped water from the basement than we find the roof leaks. After months of unemployment, we finally find a job. But two months later, layoffs drive us back to the want ads. At last, the youngest child leaves the nest to live on her own. But two months later, an older brother's divorce makes us guardians of his small children. No wonder the Bible praises patience as a Christian virtue!

Boaz proposed a plan (v. 13). Ruth would spend the rest of the night at the threshing floor. Then, the other man would get his chance: "In the morning, if he wants to redeem, good; let him redeem. But if he is not willing, I vow that, as surely as the Lord lives, I will do it." One way or the other, Ruth would have a *gō'ēl* by midmorning that day. It might be Boaz, it might be the other person. Naturally, we hope it is Boaz!

So, following Boaz's plan, the two slept (if they could!) on the threshing floor the rest of the night. The dawn would bring a settlement between Boaz and the other kinsman.

A Special Gift
Just before dawn, Ruth got up and stirred around. It was still pitch dark out because she arose "before someone could rec-

ognize someone else" (Ruth 3:14, my translation of the Heb.). That remark suggested Ruth's reason for getting up—to get back to town before anyone recognized her. She hoped that darkness would keep her return as secret as it had kept her departure.

Cleverly, the author added a touch of humor here. He used the verb "to recognize" (*nākar*) again. Ruth had rejoiced at the recognition she had received (*nākar*, 2:10, 19). Now she tried to avoid it. Though happy about getting married, she knew that it was not time to "wake the town and tell the people!"

Meanwhile, Boaz still lay on the threshing floor. Apparently, her stirring set him to thinking. He said to himself, "It must not be known that the woman came to the threshing floor" (3:14, my translation of the Heb.). He shared Ruth's concern for secrecy—and perhaps for the same reasons. Both were highly respected in Bethlehem (2:1; 3:11). Perhaps they feared that scandal might entrap them if word of their meeting got out.

As noted earlier, in the popular mind, threshing floors were where prostitutes did their business. How could the two prove that they had not met on similar business? Or, knowledge of their talk might complicate the legal proceedings to follow. The other kinsman might use that knowledge to his advantage in dealing with Boaz. Boaz sought to head off such unpleasantness. Like Naomi, he came up with a simple plan (v. 15).

First, he asked Ruth to hold out her shawl. Probably this was the large mantle which ancient women wore as a head covering. Second, he poured six measures of barley into it. We do not know the exact amount of barley given. But the fact that he helped her load up ("put it on her") implies a generous amount. Probably he placed the load on her head or over her shoulder so she could carry it home by herself. Then Boaz went back to town.

But how would the load of grain help Ruth return without being noticed? We cannot be sure, but we can make a good guess. Without the grain, people meeting Ruth might suspect immorality. After all, she was a single woman out alone at night in a suspicious locale. But with the grain load, people might assume that Ruth had worked all night—but not as a prostitute. They might conclude that she had simply worked overtime to finish her threshing.

Now notice that Ruth again obeyed. She cooperated with Boaz's plan just as she had Naomi's ("she did so," v. 15). She stretched out her shawl to Boaz. She presumed that Boaz acted to do her good and not harm. She trusted in Boaz's deep concern for her. That concern mirrors God's deep concern for His people. If Boaz cared for Ruth, how much more so the Lord cares for us!

And that is the first basis of patience we learn in this scene. Patience relies wholeheartedly on God's *concern*. As a Christian, I can be patient because I know God is always at work for me, not against me. If He fails to intervene, it is not because He does not care; it is not because He is out to get me.

Recall Paul's famous teaching: "And we know that in all things God works for the good of those who love Him, who have been called according to His purpose" (Rom. 8:28). Why? Because God's salvation plan (v. 29) proved that He is on our side (cf. v. 31). If God willingly gave up His own beloved Son, Paul argued, He certainly would not begrudge us anything else! By letting Jesus die for us, God proved His love for us. Although it's hard, we can patiently wait for God's help because we know He cares.

Some years ago, the deadly disease of dissension attacked a church I attended. Disagreements over church plans divided people into camps. One group criticized the church's leaders, another defended them. Soon the congregation became discouraged and defeated. The turmoil even drove some people from the church.

One day I shared my grief with a former member who now lived in another state. She understood what I was going through but gave me some good advice. During earlier troubles, she had angrily grieved over the situation with the pastor. "I am losing patience with all this fuss," she had told him. "I wish God would do something about it!"

Wisely, the pastor had replied, "We must remember that this is God's church. He cares more about it than anyone else." There was nothing more to be said. Since God cared, we could only wait for Him to act on His schedule. Because He cared, we knew that He would somehow work things out.

In trouble, it is tempting to doubt that God cares. It is easy to lose patience with what we see as His slow reaction time. Our human nature wants to push the accelerator to the floor and take action. A patient Christian, however, wants to please God. So, she waits for God to intervene. She trusts that, despite appearances, God wants what is best for us. Such a Christian believes that God's inactivity may actually be an expression of His concern.

An End to Emptiness

As Ruth and Boaz talked, back in Bethlehem Naomi waited and wondered. Imagine what a night she must have had! I doubt that she got much sleep. Probably she waited and waited as minute after painful minute passed. Nervously, she may have paced the floor and earnestly prayed. Perhaps to calm her nerves, her mind reviewed the plan to approach Boaz again and again. Each review reassured her—until doubts seized her again.

At the same time, her ears kept listening for the sound of Ruth's footsteps. Occasionally perhaps, she secretly peered out the door to see if Ruth might be coming up the street. She may even have heard Boaz's predawn return to town. That would have ignited Naomi's excitement—and her curiosity!

Meanwhile, keeping her distance, Ruth followed Boaz back to the city (Ruth 3:16). Excitedly, Naomi welcomed her, asking, "How did it go?" Had the plan succeeded or not? Was Ruth now married to Boaz? Quickly, Ruth "told her everything Boaz had done for her" (v. 16). Through that summary, Naomi learned the details which we already witnessed.

Then, however, the author paused over one important detail—a detail, in fact, reported in verses 15-16. According to

Ruth, as Boaz gave the grain he commented, "Don't go back to your mother-in-law empty-handed" (v. 17). Why did the author purposely save that comment for special mention here? Evidently, he wanted to underscore the significance of the gift. To be specific, he wanted us to hear the word "empty-handed" (*rêqām*) again.

The last time we heard it was from Naomi's lips. In 1:21, she said, "I went away full, but the Lord has brought me back empty (*rêqām*)." The context was Naomi's bitter outcry against God for her tragic life. Her emptiness involved two things she lacked, food and an heir. In 3:17, the context was a grain gift, and the speaker was Boaz. "Don't go empty-handed (*rêqām*) to your mother-in-law."

By hearing the word again, we recall Naomi's earlier use of it. That, in turn, sets the two scenes side-by-side in our minds, letting us compare them. By mentally comparing them, we see how this scene provided the solution—at least in part—to the problems of Ruth 1.

Now the thematic importance of the word "empty-handed" becomes clear. Through the grain, Boaz reassured Naomi that she would have enough food. This resolved the first aspect of Naomi's emptiness (cf. v. 1). The abundant quantity of grain promised that Ruth and Naomi would not go hungry. At the same time, the grain probably promised a solution to the second emptiness—Naomi's lack of an heir. Ancient readers would have recognized the grain as a symbol of "seed" or offspring.

So, the gift promised Naomi that Ruth would have a husband soon. Her marriage would give Naomi the chance to have an heir. As one writer put it, "The seed to fill the stomach was promise of the seed to fill the womb."[7] In sum, the simple gift of grain symbolized that God-given fullness was about to replace Naomi's tragic emptiness.

Now this teaches us the second basis of patience: patience relies on God's *commitment* to us. It banks on God's promises of help. With confidence, we can endure painful circumstances because we know God is for us (Rom. 8:31). With contentment, we can wait out any storm because we know that God will not let it overwhelm us. He has committed Himself to stand with us, to defend us, and to supply us.

Judah's King Hezekiah experienced that. During his reign, the great empire of Assyria ruled the Near East. Annually, its mighty army marched from Mesopotamia to control and expand the empire. One of its victims was Israel, the Northern Kingdom. The Assyrians completely destroyed it in 722 B.C. (2 Kings 17:1-41). In 701 B.C., Assyria destroyed all Judah's main cities and threatened even to destroy Jerusalem (18:13-19).

Hezekiah found himself trapped in the capital like a bird in a cage. Outside, Assyrian officers ridiculed Judean resistance, reviled her reliance on God, and recommended immediate surrender (vv. 19-35). By all appearances, it was only a matter of time before the full fury of the Assyrian army would demolish the city.

A lesser man than Hezekiah would have panicked. Hezekiah, however, went to the temple and prayed (19:14-19). He asked God to deliver His people. Through the Prophet Isaiah, God promised to defend Jerusalem (v. 34). The Assyrians would not get inside the city. They would not even get off a shot against her! Instead, they would make a surprising retreat (vv. 32-33).

Notice one reason God gave for His salvation. He would act "for the sake of David My servant." God had made a commitment to His loyal servant David and He would honor it (see Ps. 132:11-18). For David's sake, Jerusalem would be saved. So Hezekiah waited to see Jerusalem's deliverance.

He did not wait long. That very night the Angel of the Lord swept through the Assyrian camp (vv. 35-36). Nearly 200,000 soldiers died. Assyria's King Sennacherib broke camp, returned to Nineveh, his capital, and stayed there. Jerusalem was saved! It was a salvation worth waiting for! And so is ours.

Do you feel surrounded by your troubles? Do you wonder when God will deliver you? Remember, God is just as committed to you as He was to Hezekiah and Jerusalem. Though modern-day Assyrians assault us, God is on our side. He only asks that we patiently await His help.

Yes, sometimes we must wait longer than Ruth or Hezekiah did. Indeed, God may ask us to wait years—perhaps even until Jesus returns—before He intervenes. But however long the wait, we wait with confidence in God's commitment to us. When He does act, His action will be total and final. He will bring our waiting to an end.

A Man of Action

Naomi had advised Ruth how to respond to Boaz (see Ruth 2:22). Now she counseled, "Wait [lit. sit], my daughter, until you find out what happens." Boaz now held the reins in his hands. His actions would determine Ruth's destiny. There was nothing Ruth could do now but sit tight.

Ruth was not accustomed to sitting tight. She had firmly insisted on coming with Naomi to Bethlehem in the first place (1:16-17). She took the initiative to provide them food by gleaning (2:2). She boldly carried out Naomi's risky plan to arrange her marriage to Boaz as a *gō'ēl*. Clearly, she had been one of the story's main "movers and shakers."

Now, however, Boaz would do the moving and shaking. She could only wait to see how his moving would shake down for her. Certainly, Naomi could sympathize with any impatience by Ruth. Ruth was about to taste a little of what Naomi had just gone through the previous night!

Boaz had promised to take care of things. But what assurance did Ruth have that he would? Was there a chance that he might wait a day or so? After further reflection, might he even change his mind?

Yes, she had his word that he would act "in the morning" (3:13). But maybe he just said that to be polite. Maybe he knew it would take more time but he was too embarrassed to tell her. If so, the wait might be long—perhaps longer than poor Naomi's! That would be pure agony for poor Ruth.

Naomi, however, reassured her. That was certainly appropriate. Naomi had gotten her into this situation. And it was Naomi who knew Boaz best. I suspect Naomi factored in her knowledge of him when preparing her plan. Drawing on that knowledge again, Naomi assured Ruth of her confidence in Boaz. With him in charge, Ruth would certainly be married that very day.

Why was Naomi so confident? She said, "For the man will not rest until the matter is settled today" (v. 18). In Hebrew, "rest" is actually the verb "to be quiet, inactive" (*shāqaṭ*). In Isaiah 18:4, it described God as quiet—a passive, unemotional spectator watching the coming judgment from the heavenly sidelines. In Psalm 83:1, the psalmist used it to plead for God not to sit quietly by while his enemies plotted to destroy Israel.

So, "to be quiet" meant here "to relax, to stop striving." According to Naomi, that was what Boaz would *not* do. He would not take so much as a coffee break until the job was done.

It was the character of Boaz which inspired Naomi's confidence. He was a man who kept his word—what he promised he did. He was completely trustworthy. Ruth could safely entrust her fate into his hands. Whatever he did would be in Ruth's best interest. Further, he was a man who followed through immediately. He would not dillydally around. No other matters would distract his attention or divert his efforts.

On the contrary, his path would not swerve from its goal. He would not relax until he had settled the matter. The Jewish Midrash offers an insightful comment on Boaz here: "The yes of the righteous is yes, and their no, no." Boaz reminds us of the kind of people we should be—people whose word is good as gold, people who follow through.

More important, Boaz also reminds us about God's character. If Boaz was trustworthy, how much more so the Lord Himself! Indeed, here we see the final basis for patience—the *character* of God. Our patience rests secure on the character of God. Specifically, God is true to His word.

Consider the case of King Balak of Moab. Israel wanted to pass through Moab en route to the Promised Land. But Israel so outnumbered Moab that poor Balak was terrified. Israel could do terrible damage to his kingdom (Num. 22:2-4). So he asked Balaam the prophet to curse Israel. But Balaam said that God had blessed Israel—and the blessing still stood. He told Balak: "God is not a man that He should lie, nor a son of man, that He should change His mind. Does He speak and then not act? Does He promise and not fulfill?" (Num. 23:19)

What God says He will do, He does. Unlike us, He is never moody or impulsive. He does not run "hot" one day and "cold" the next. No, His character remains consistent. That means that He stands behind all His promises to us. When we call, He never answers, "Oh, I don't feel like doing that today." He always responds, though He always follows His own timetable.

That is why one Christian could write, drawing on Lamentations 3:22-23:

Great is Thy faithfulness, O God my Father!
There is no shadow of turning with Thee.
Thou changest not, Thy compassions they fail not;
As Thou hast been, Thou forever wilt be.*

That is the character of our God—steadfast, loyal, unchanging. His character frees us, like Ruth, to relax and wait. We relax because God, like Boaz, does not. His character is one reason we can patiently wait.

The Waiting Game

"Daddy, are we there yet?" my son asked as our car hummed along the interstate. He had no idea the trip had hardly begun! But we are all like that. When we want something to happen, we want it *now*. We want to rev up the engine, pop the clutch, and get moving. To ask us to wait patiently is like asking us to fly without an airplane. Impossible!

But God's work in our lives is like the familiar traffic signal

---

*"Great Is Thy Faithfulness,"
Words: Thomas O. Chisholm

at busy intersections. At times, God gives us the "Go" sign. He opens a clear path before us with clear directions to proceed. Naomi certainly saw that sign in Boaz's kindness to Ruth. So she moved ahead by sending Ruth to the threshing floor. When we see God's "Go," we go ahead too.

At other times, God flashes us the "Wait" sign. He leaves us no open door, clears no path, and provides no direction. Ruth saw that sign as Boaz headed to town to meet the other relative. She could do nothing but sit tight and await the outcome. And so, at times, must we. To ignore God's "Wait" sign means we might be run over by the results of our disobedience.

God asks for our patience. He asks that we trust His concern for us. He wants us to rely completely on His firm commitment to us. He desires that we bank on His trustworthy character. He asks that we believe that His timing is always perfect—that He will act at exactly the right moment.

The famous missionary Dr. Hudson Taylor often shared his burden for China with church groups. Many young people expressed an interest in joining his ministry. But years in China had taught Taylor what Christian witness there required. So he always gave eager volunteers some wise advice.

He warned them that there were three absolutely indispensable requirements for a missionary:

1. Patience.
2. Patience.
3. Patience.

That is also a quality of faithfulness which God would like to see in us. Yes, at times it is the hardest thing in the world to do. Our pain is so intense. We do not know if we can hold on much longer. Our frustration seems about ready to boil over. We feel like we are about to explode.

Has God flashed you the "Wait" sign? Whatever your difficulty, follow Ruth's patient example. God has not abandoned you. He is at work. He will sustain you. One day, He will change things. Until then, God wants you to show simple patience. He wants you simply to wait.

Chapter Eleven

Integrity: Faithfulness Honors Law

Ruth 4:1-12

On October 28, 1987 Santa Claus paid a surprise visit to Columbus, Ohio. About 9:30 that morning, an armored truck sped through town on Interstate 71. Suddenly, the back door flew open and bags of money spilled along the highway. A million dollars in cash rained down on a mile of the roadway.

Soon, motorists realized the windfall was not maple leaves but money. They quickly braked and jumped out to pile cash into their cars. The news spread by CB radio. Immediately, hundreds of people—some from across town—came to help clean up. People stuffed bills into pockets and purses and left, celebrating their good fortune.

What lack of integrity! People claimed "finders keepers, losers weepers." The "finders" rejected offers of substantial rewards for returned money. One "keeper" even bragged that he was now set for life and was leaving town. Of the million dollars lost, only $100,000 came back. Apparently, people only saw themselves as very lucky. They never considered that they were thieves.

These days, lawbreaking makes front page news in other unlikely places. Evil has ensnared leaders of all ranks—businessmen, members of Congress, mayors, police chiefs, and attorneys. Once wealthy stockbrokers now share prison cells with ordinary robbers and rapists. Meanwhile, businesses complain about theft of company property by their employees. Every year, the losses mount into millions of dollars.

Corruption has even snagged well-known religious leaders. As I write, one sits in prison convicted of crimes while another struggles to salvage his ministry from public shame. Integrity seems to be in short supply. Dishonesty infects people at all levels of society from leaders to followers.

The Bible itself diagnoses the causes of this shortage. King David's adultery with Bathsheba illustrates one reason (2 Sam. 11). David slept with Bathsheba while her husband was away at war. Then he tried to cover up the crime by arranging her husband's death in combat. The reason David sinned was that he had an inflated view of himself. As king, he thought he was so important that he did not have to play by the rules.

Many people today show that same wrong sense of self-importance. They love to throw their weight around or name-drop, mentioning all the famous people they know. They brag about their influence in high places. Their favorite song is, "How Great I Art!" Like David, they believe their importance exempts them from obeying ethical rules so they cut ethical corners.

About 630 B.C., the Prophet Zephaniah gave a second reason for people's lack of integrity. They do not believe God will hold them accountable for their actions. Zephaniah summed up Jerusalem's smug attitude: "The Lord will do nothing, either good or bad" (Zeph. 1:12). In other words, Jerusalem thought she could live any way she wanted because God would do nothing.

I sense a similar attitude among many people today. They live as if God did not exist. They behave as if God will never hold them accountable. They pooh-pooh the idea that God might punish their wickedness through terrible events. They laugh at the thought of a final judgment before God. They live as they please, breaking ethical rules whenever they please.

Boaz, however, presents a refreshing alternative. He had promised to settle Ruth's marital status right away (Ruth 3:13). In this scene, we will watch how he handled the matter. He modeled integrity in action. Indeed, by watching him, we will learn three aspects of true, biblical integrity.

The City Gate

The midnight talk between Boaz and Ruth had been a private one. The marriage of a widow to a kinsman-redeemer, however, was a public matter. To be valid, the parties had to follow proper legal procedure. That another relative had a legal right to Ruth made a legal settlement even more necessary. A public process in court was the only way that Bethlehem would recognize Ruth's marriage.

So, that very morning Boaz went to the city gate (Ruth 4:1). In ancient cities, the city gate was more than just an opening in the wall with giant wooden doors. One should actually call it the "city gate area." It was a large, open space between a town's inner and outer walls.

Since city streets were narrow, the gate area served as a kind of central town square. It provided the best place for people to gather. There vendors hawked their wares and citizens swapped stories. Most important, it served as the town courthouse, the place to settle legal matters. There, towns held criminal trials and resolved legal disputes (Deut. 21:19; Josh. 20:4). That is why Boaz went there to arrange Ruth's marriage.

Boaz had a stroke of good luck (or shall we call it God's providence?). He reached the gate shortly after dawn. Probably early morning "rush hour" traffic clogged the city gate. Noisy chatter filled the air as merchants set up shop, farmers set out for the fields, and traders left on business.

Boaz arrived just in time. The other kinsman-redeemer soon passed by in the crowd. "Come over here, my friend, and sit down," Boaz cried out over the noise (Ruth 4:1). Since Boaz had a legal matter to settle, "sit down" may have meant something like "sit in legal session." If so, Boaz's word choice signaled that the two had business to do. That may be why the relative came right over to Boaz and sat down.

Next, Boaz drew ten elders from the crowd (v. 2). In ancient Israel, elders were the leaders of a given city's main families. Together they formed the town government (Jud. 8:16; 1 Sam. 11:3). Israel prized their wisdom (Jer. 26:17). In this case, Boaz tapped their knowledge of Israelite legal practice. Their duty was to make certain that the judicial process about to unfold was legal (see Ruth 4:9, 11).

Bethlehem probably had many more than ten elders (see Jud. 8:14). So the "ten" probably formed a kind of quorum — the minimum number required for a meeting to be official. The elders sat down beside Boaz and the other kinsman. All parties to the case — the two kinsmen and the presiding authorities — were now present.

Let me explain the legal process. This was not a trial to decide guilt or innocence, but an administrative procedure. There were no attorneys, no witnesses, and no verdict or penalty. Rather, it was like a modern adoption hearing. Such a hearing seeks to establish the legal rights and responsibilities of the new parents. Its gives the parents the legal basis for doing their job.

Similarly, in Ruth 4, the legal issue was the right to serve as *gō'ēl* for Naomi and Ruth. By being the closest relative, the first man owned that right. The hearing was to decide whether he would exercise it or waive it. If he waived it, Boaz stood ready to step in.

Here Boaz modeled the first aspect of integrity — he acted with open honesty. Boaz might have made a backroom deal to get what he wanted. Like anyone, the other man probably had his price. A nice sum of money or an attractive piece of property could have won his cooperation in court. Both the man and Boaz would be happy, and no one else would be the wiser.

Or, if the man would not cooperate, Boaz had other means of getting his way. He might have quietly used his influence with the elders. If necessary, Boaz could have bribed them to find some "legal" way to arrange things. Bribery was as common back then as it is today. People who work under the table usually get what they want.

King Ahab's wife, Jezebel, was such a person (see 1 Kings 21). Once, her husband wanted a vineyard which bordered his land. But its owner, an Israelite named Naboth, refused to deal with Ahab. The land was Naboth's ancestral property. Legally it had to remain in his family's hands. Not even the king could get Naboth to disobey the law.

So Jezebel got some people to falsely accuse Naboth of terrible crimes. A kangaroo court convicted Naboth and had him executed. Then Ahab got what he wanted, thanks to his cruel wife. Yes, people who bend the rules usually get what they want.

Boaz, however, was no Jezebel. He followed Israelite law to the letter. He took the matter to court in the town square. He did everything in public, before the town officials, not in secret. The whole town would know what had taken place. No one would suspect shady dealings. By going public, Boaz proved that he was a man of the highest integrity.

His example calls Christians to be people of similar integrity—people whose honesty no one doubts. Here some words from the Apostle Paul point us in the right direction. Paul spoke about how integrity in spreading the Gospel verified the truth of the Good News. His words, however, sound like a Christian motto of integrity: "We have renounced secret and shameful ways; we do not use deception, nor do we distort the Word of God. On the contrary, by setting forth the truth plainly we commend ourselves to every [one's] conscience in the sight of God" (2 Cor. 4:2; cf. Acts 26:26). In sum, integrity is one way Christians show their faithfulness to Christ. By living honest, transparent lives before our neighbors we honor Him. That is the example Boaz gives us.

The Right to Ruth

The city officials, Boaz, and his relative sat at the gate. Now the official proceedings began. Unexpectedly, however, Boaz sprang a surprise. We expected him to arrange a marriage for Ruth as he promised. Instead, he brought up a field which Naomi wanted to sell (Ruth 4:3). He said nothing about Ruth at all!

That strikes us as a surprise because the book never mentions the field or Naomi's desire to sell it. The surprise also

134

frustrates us. We were ready to hear wedding bells ring for Ruth and Boaz. Now Boaz wants to haggle over property!

There were two good legal reasons, however, for Boaz to bring up the matter. First, sooner or later Naomi's relatives would have to decide who would get the land. The property was Elimelech's inheritance—land passed down to him from his ancestors. Naomi had temporary custody of it (see Num. 27:1-11; 36:1-12; 2 Kings 8:1-6). Israelite law required that such land remain in the family. Since Naomi had no children to inherit it, ownership would have to go to someone else.

Second, as a *gō'ēl*, Boaz had a duty to bring up the matter. The Israelite *gō'ēl* was responsible for helping weak family members. He also was to make sure that property stayed in the family (see Lev. 25:25-28). Apparently, Boaz thought that this was as good a time as any to settle the issue. Of course, should Naomi somehow get an heir, the heir would inherit the land.

So Boaz asked the other man to buy—that is, to take over—Elimelech's land (Ruth 4:4). He was to "redeem" it— that is, as a *gō'ēl*, to own it on behalf of the family. If he declined the duty, Boaz added, he himself was the next nearest relative. He stood ready to redeem it himself. The other man agreed to take the land over.

The decision made good sense. To serve as *gō'ēl* might enhance his reputation in Bethlehem. Everyone would admire him as a loyal family man. Also, the extra property would reap him extra profits each year—and at little or no cost. It was an offer the man could not refuse!

No sooner had he agreed, however, than Boaz sprang another surprise. At least, it surprised his relative. Boaz finally came to the subject of Ruth. He told the man that Ruth went with the land (v. 5). To possess the property meant he had to marry Ruth.

Also, Boaz spelled out the purpose for this added requirement—"to maintain the name of the dead with his property." To explain this, we must review some background given earlier (see chapter 9). As I pointed out, Israel had a unique view of afterlife. She believed that, after death, Israelites lived on in their descendants.

So, to die without children was a great tragedy. Without children, the family line could not continue. That is why Naomi's situation was so terrible. When she died, there was no one to keep Elimelech's family line alive. It would simply vanish.

To prevent that tragedy, Israel allowed a brother or a close relative (i.e., a *gō'ēl)* to marry the widow and give the dead relative an heir (see Gen. 38; Deut. 25:5-10). In this case, Ruth substituted for the widow Naomi since Naomi was too old to bear children. Let me, however, add one other point not mentioned earlier.

Notice the words of Ruth 4:5 – "to maintain the name of the dead with his property." The newborn heir was to inherit the property of his dead ancestor. Evidently, Israel thought that the dead lived on in their descendants *and* on their property. In other words, to keep the dead alive, their heirs had to own the family's ancestral land.

That was the principle which Boaz invoked here. So, the *gō'ēl* had to do more than just take over the land. He was duty bound to marry Ruth, Naomi's substitute. He was obliged to give Elimelech an heir to inherit the property – or at least to make the attempt.

Cold Feet

Suddenly, the deal struck the fellow as a loser. It was no longer just a cheap way to win popularity and make some easy money. The bottom line had shifted from the black into the red. The man quickly backpedaled (Ruth 4:6): "I cannot redeem it because I might endanger my own estate."

Now, why would serving as *gō'ēl* "endanger" the man's estate? Perhaps he saw the potential expense involved. He would have three additional people to feed and clothe – Naomi, Ruth, and, possibly, the heir. Were Ruth to bear him other children, he would have to bear their expenses too. Also, those children might be entitled to inherit some of the man's own estate. If so, each of his heirs would receive a smaller piece of it than before.

Or perhaps he was just making an excuse. Perhaps he

136

simply did not want to complicate his life. He probably already had a wife and kids. Maybe the thought of adding a second wife and more kids to the family made him uneasy. Maybe he did not think the rescue of Naomi was really worth the extra trouble. He could not give the real reason, of course—he would look bad in front of everyone.

So he gave a nice-sounding excuse. All this talk about "endanger[ing] my own estate" may have amounted to a polite "I just cannot afford this." Whatever his reason, the point was that he refused to serve as *gō'ēl*. He waived his right in favor of Boaz. "You redeem it yourself," he told Boaz (v. 6). With him out of the picture, Boaz was free to take his place.

Now notice the contrast between these two men. The other relative was willing to take but not to give. He was happy to benefit from Naomi's field but not to sacrifice for Ruth and Naomi. They were just too much trouble for him. Boaz, on the other hand, gladly took on what the other man refused. He was willing to take responsibility for them. He was happy to make the sacrifice necessary to benefit them.

Here Boaz modeled a second aspect of Christian integrity. A person of integrity will pay any price to do what is right. The cold, hard truth is that integrity costs. It requires self-sacrifice and effort. It demands that one take on, not avoid, troubles. The price tag for doing what is right is usually high. It was for Boaz. He had to support Naomi, Ruth, and any children born to them. But he willingly paid the price.

Ted Williams, one of baseball's greatest hitters, paid that same price. In 1959, a painful pinched nerve in his neck made batting almost impossible. For the first time, the great slugger hit below .300—a miserable .254 average. But he still earned $125,000, the highest salary in sports.

Graciously, the Red Sox offered Williams the same contract for the next season. But he insisted on taking a $35,000 pay cut for his poor performance. Said Williams, "They were offering me a contract I did not deserve."

To do what is right costs. Sometimes the cost is in dollars and cents. Other times one pays in the coin of effort and risk. Integrity often demands that we admit a mistake or own up to

doing a wrong. In such cases, there is often a painful sur-
charge—humility or embarrassment. Whatever the cost, a
Christian of integrity willingly pays the bill just as Boaz did.

Making Everything Legal

Someone said, "Integrity means we do all the things that we
tell others to do." In other words, we live by the same rules
we expect others to obey. A person of integrity, Boaz did
exactly what he had asked his relative to do. He officially took
on the duty of *gōʾēl* in a formal, legal transaction.

Every society has procedures for making such transac-
tions. Today, signatures on written documents, sometimes
properly notarized, complete deals. For example, to sell a car
one signs over the vehicle title to the new owner. The state
then registers the car and issues a title in the new owner's
name.

As Ruth 4:7 notes, however, early Israel did not use written, notarized documents. That practice came later (see
Deut. 24:1-4; Isa. 10:1-2; Jer. 32:10). Instead, to transfer ownership, the old owner took off his sandal and handed it to the
new one, symbolizing the transfer of ownership from one
person to the other.

In fact, the ancient world commonly associated feet with
ownership. Texts found at Nuzi in Mesopotamia report a similar example. To transfer ownership of property, the old owner lifted up his foot from the land and put the new owner's
foot on it. Likewise, in Israel to "set foot" on property meant
to own it (Deut. 11:24; Josh. 14:9). Some scholars even think
that by walking throughout Canaan, Abraham was laying legal
claim to it (Gen. 13; 17).

So, when Boaz's relative handed him his sandal (Ruth 4:8),
he publicly gave his rights as *gōʾēl* to Boaz. Solemnly, he told
Boaz, "Buy it yourself." Legally, the man was, to borrow a
phrase, off the hook. Now Boaz was free to exercise those
rights—to do what his fellow kinsman had refused to do. He
could buy the field and marry Ruth.

Boaz wasted no time. Immediately, he turned to address
the elders and the crowd of onlookers. Notice how much

detail his long statement covers (vv. 9-10). Just as we make sure a bill of sale lists everything bought, so Boaz carefully listed everything that had been settled. His statement amounted to a precise legal contract in words.

First, he used standard wording expected by Israelite legal practice: "Today you are witnesses" (see Josh. 24:22; 1 Sam. 12:5; Isa. 43:9-12). Should anyone dispute the deal in the future, the people who witnessed it would verify what had happened. In other words, their memory would play the role a written contract does today.

Second, Boaz itemized what the transaction covered. As of that moment, he took over from Naomi "all the property of Elimelech, Kilion and Mahlon" (Ruth 4:9). This included not only the field, but everything else owned by the family. By the way, this was the first time that the book has mentioned all of Elimelech's family since chapter 1 (see v. 2). Their mention hinted that the book's main tragedy, the end of Elimelech's family line, was about to end.

Next, Boaz claimed Ruth as his wife (4:10). His words sound almost dramatic, as if he was bringing the scene to its climax. Boaz described her with legal precision as well— "Ruth the Moabitess, Mahlon's widow." Of course, as readers we cheer this moment. It is just what we have been waiting for since the couple first met in chapter 2!

Then Boaz restated the purpose of this marriage—to keep Elimelech's family line alive. Any child born to him and Ruth would serve as the dead man's heir. He would indeed keep Elimelech, Mahlon, and Kilion alive on their ancestral land. To finish the contract, Boaz restated the legal phrase, "Today you are witnesses!"

Following Israelite custom, the crowd responded, "We are witnesses" (4:11). The people accepted responsibility for verifying the transaction in the future. At that moment, it became legal. Now Elimelech's entire estate and the widow Ruth belonged to Boaz.

More important, the event brought several of the book's themes to a climax. It answered Ruth's request to marry a *gōʾēl* to benefit Naomi. In the process, God finally gave Ruth the two things Naomi and Boaz had prayed for earlier. She now had rest—a "place of settled security" (see 1:8-9; 3:1) and her full reward (see 2:12).

Also, by becoming Boaz's wife, Ruth probably attained full status as an Israelite. That showed that God, indeed, accepted foreigners into His people. In that regard, the Book of Ruth anticipated the spread of the Gospel to all nations (see Matt. 28:19-20; Acts 1:8).

The Reward: A Blessing

The legal proceedings concluded on a very upbeat note. Joyfully, the crowd pronounced a beautiful blessing on Ruth and Boaz (Ruth 4:11). It is uncertain whether Israelite legal processes regularly ended with such blessings. Perhaps the practice only applied to cases involving marriage (see Gen. 24:60; Ps. 45:17).

In any case, the people first asked the Lord to grant Ruth many children. God was to make her "like Rachel and Leah." In other words, the crowd prayed that Ruth would become one of Israel's "founding mothers," a woman of great importance to the entire nation. What a great destiny for a mere Moabite!

Next, the crowd prayed that Boaz would enjoy two happy results from Ruth's fertility. First, Boaz would "have standing in Ephratah" (probably Bethlehem's ancient name). In Hebrew, "have standing" literally reads "to make power." Here it probably meant "to prosper financially." In short, when Ruth had many kids, Boaz would prosper.

Now, to us that connection sounds strange. The more children we have, the greater the strain on our family budget! Bethlehem, however, was a farming community. A large family provided more workers for the fields. The more workers, the greater the harvest. So the more kids, the greater one's prosperity.

Second, Boaz would "become famous [lit. make a name] in Bethlehem." Again, the connection between many children and fame does not ring a bell with us. Probably the people meant that having many well-respected children would enhance Boaz's own reputation in the town.

Finally, they sought a special blessing on Boaz's family line (Ruth 4:12). They prayed that God would make it "like that of Perez, whom Tamar bore to Judah." Perez was the son of Judah from whom Boaz and most of Bethlehem descended. (For his unusual birth, see Gen. 38).

Biblical genealogies show that the line of Perez became the leading family of the tribe of Judah (see 46:12; Num. 26:20-21; 1 Chron. 2:3-6; 4:1). In short, the crowd wished that Boaz and Ruth establish a similarly important family in Judah. Again, what a great future destiny!

Now, we all know that people pass out may-God-bless-yous almost without thinking. That phrase is simply a religious way of saying, "Have a nice day." Is the blessing of Ruth and Boaz just a polite, well-meant formality not to be taken seriously? The answer is no. Notice several important things.

First, the blessing wishes that the couple found a large, influential family line. Clearly, the well-wishers had in mind something much greater than just an heir for Elimelech. They hoped that this marriage might spawn a leading Judean family. As we shall see, the blessing proved to be almost prophetic! In fact, I think the author included it to prepare us for the surprise he intended to spring in Ruth 4:17.

Second, the blessing paid fitting tribute to the scene's hero, Boaz. The gathered crowd almost sounded like a great choir singing his praise. After all, unlike the other relative, Boaz lived out his loyalty to the family. At some personal cost, he took custody of Elimelech's estate in hopes of passing it on to an heir.

He also took on the care of Naomi, Ruth, and any children born to them. In essence, the crowd's blessing was a hymn of praise to his remarkable dedication. It also reminds us of a third aspect of integrity. Integrity may cost, but it also pays great rewards. By his actions, Boaz had earned the praise of all Bethlehem. And, as we shall see in the next chapter, the best was yet to come!

William E. Gladstone was an English political statesman who lived in the nineteenth century. His deep Christian faith shaped his politics. Gladstone served many years in the British parliament and four terms as prime minister. The highly respected Baptist preacher, Charles Spurgeon, lived at the same time as Gladstone. Spurgeon once said of Gladstone, "We believe in no man's infallibility, but it is restful to feel sure of one man's integrity."

That is one reward of integrity—the respect and trust of others. Neighbors always steer clear of anyone they do not respect or trust. But they feel secure and comfortable around someone whose integrity they admire. That is why the people in Bethlehem praised Boaz—he was a man of integrity. Bethlehem's praise was his reward. If we follow his example, we will enjoy similar rewards. Integrity pays handsomely.

Conclusion

Sadly, integrity is in short supply today. Scandals of greed, corruption, and immorality fill the news. People prefer to cut ethical corners than to live honestly. Employees rob their employers of supplies and of a good day's work. Employers push employee production to satisfy company greed for gain. Back scratching, backstabbing, and back-room dealings are the order of the day.

Leaders seem more like caterers than leaders. They regard people more as "customers" than followers. They prefer pleasing them to leading them. They would rather waffle on an issue than take an unpopular stand. They spend more time polishing their image than standing for what is right. We could use another Boaz.

We could also use another Henry David Thoreau. Thoreau was an American writer who lived in the nineteenth century. His essay "Civil Disobedience" called for the abolition of slavery. He went to jail rather than pay his poll tax to a state which supported slavery. According to a popular story, Thoreau's good friend, Ralph Waldo Emerson, came to visit him in jail.

Peering through the bars, Emerson exclaimed, "Why, Henry, what are you doing in there?" Looking back, Thoreau replied, "Nay, Ralph, the question is, what are you doing out there?" (Robert Burleigh, *A Man Named Thoreau* [New York: Atheneum, 1985], 24)

Like Boaz, Thoreau lived honestly. He paid the price for his integrity. The question was whether Emerson would join him in living with integrity. Any Christian who desires to live for God faithfully must answer the question Thoreau asked Emerson, "What are you doing?" Does biblical integrity characterize your life? If not, what can you do to change that?

You might confess to God any dishonesty which troubles you. Let Him clean it out of your life. Then ask God to show you how to live like Boaz—as a person of integrity.

Chapter Twelve
Celebration: Faithfulness Reaps the Harvest
Ruth 4:13-17

Our family loves to celebrate. It is part of our family tradition. Completion of a major milestone always calls for some festivity. When my first book came out, we all went out to dinner. A year later, it won an award, so we went out to eat again.

When my wife turned forty, we threw her two big parties — one at home and one in the town where she grew up. When she got her first job, we really did it up big. We hit our favorite restaurant, then bought a new car!

Our family also celebrates small victories. In elementary school, our two boys played on basketball teams. The games never had record-breaking scores since the kids had trouble just hefting the heavy ball through the hoop. But I promised my two players a donut for any basket they scored. As I remember, they each averaged about one donut per game!

Years later, when our oldest son got a new job, we all went out for dessert. We did the same when our youngest son aced a big test. At our house, we celebrate birthdays, anniversaries, good grades, and special achievements.

The Bible recognizes the value of celebrations. Every year, Israel held three major feasts — Passover (or Unleavened Bread), Weeks (or Pentecost), and Tabernacles (or Booths; see Ex. 23:14-16; Lev. 23; Deut. 16:1-17). Israelites from all over came to Jerusalem to celebrate. The feasts involved great processions, joyous singing, and many sacrifices.

Celebration

To call the three events "feasts" is entirely appropriate. The sacrifices were really huge community barbecues. The sweet scent of cooked meat hung heavily over Jerusalem. After burning parts of animals to the Lord, the Israelites ate the rest. During those days, the sounds of singing and laughter echoed through the city (see Isa. 30:29; Amos 5:21-23; Nahum 1:15).

Notice, however, that each feast served a purpose. Passover reminded Israel of her salvation—her rescue by God from slavery in Egypt. At the end of the grain harvest, the Feast of Weeks celebrated God's generous provision of barley and wheat. The Feast of Tabernacles recalled how God had guided and protected Israel while she lived in the wilderness.

In Bible times, families also marked special occasions with celebrations. Israel responded to special blessings with thank offerings at the temple (Lev. 7:12-15; Ps. 107:22; Jer. 17:26). People praised God for healings, rescue from trouble, the birth of a child, and answers to prayer. A wedding was also a time of special joy and feasting (Jer. 16:8-9). The return of a wayward child was reason enough to throw a big party (Luke 15:23-24).

Why make a big deal of such things? The first reason is a purely human one. Celebrations add joy to the humdrum routine of life—the kind of life most of us live. They make life more enjoyable by providing variety. Second, celebrations allow us to recognize people special to us. All of us enjoy giving—and getting—a few strokes or extra attention. So festivities give us all a chance to give and to receive such special notice.

Finally, celebrations offer us a chance to praise God for His goodness. Christians know that God's steady hand upholds us every day. He keeps us alive each year and backs our endeavors. In hard times, He provides us the strength to persevere and the courage to go on. Celebrations thank God for all He has done.

Further, they remind us that God rewards our faithfulness to Him. However meager our efforts, however feeble our attempts, He honors them. All our successes—a teacher's praise, a neighbor's thanks, a "well done" from the boss, a child's "I love you"—are His reward for living a life pleasing to God.

We discussed the reason back in chapter 1. A life of faithfulness works like seeds. To do things which honor God is like planting seeds in God's garden. Once planted, the Great Gardener gently tends them. Soon they sprout, flourish, and bear fruit. A cranky neighbor we befriended softens up. Those squirmy Sunday School kids pay more attention. A foul-mouthed coworker listens more attentively to our Christian witness.

These "successes" reflect the blessing of God on our lives—the harvest sown by seeds of faithfulness. Of course, only God can decide when and how to reward us. Some of us may only see the harvest in heaven. Others may enjoy a bumper crop on earth. God is a Gardener, not a vending machine. He decides when and how we reap the harvest. After all, He always knows what is best for us.

This brings us to Ruth and Naomi. When I began this book, I said that the Book of Ruth teaches us an important truth—that God uses the faithfulness of ordinary people to do great things for Him. So far, we have followed the fate of the two widows. We have seen God honor their faithfulness by providing them food to eat and a husband for Ruth.

It is the book's final scene (Ruth 4:13-17), however, which reports the joyous celebration of God's blessing. It also displays the full harvest of their faithfulness. More important, it springs one final, climactic surprise—one pulled by God Himself. In the process, the events remind us of four reasons to celebrate God's work in our lives.

The Last Dark Cloud

At last, the moment we have been waiting for! While Boaz was in court, Ruth had patiently awaited the outcome with Naomi (Ruth 3:18). The wait was surely worth it. Once everything was legal, Boaz got Ruth and took her home to be his wife (4:13). He made love to his new wife. (Some versions omit this, though the Hebrew original says it.)

146

So, the book's love story reached a happy end. The book could have ended satisfactorily right here. But one crucial matter remained unfinished. However marvelous the marriage, Elimelech's family line still had no heir. Unless the newlyweds produced a son, the line would cease to exist when Naomi died. All Naomi's hopes hung on their fertility. Ruth's marriage to Mahlon yielded no children (see 1:4-5). Would infertility doom this family?

That would give the book a bittersweet ending. Ruth had gained a husband, but Naomi would have lost everything. And what about the seeds of faithfulness which Naomi, Ruth, and Boaz sowed earlier? Would God, the Loving Gardener, nurse them into harvest or leave them stillborn in the ground?

What a relief! "The Lord enabled her to conceive," the Bible writer continued, "and she gave birth to a son." At last, Naomi had an heir! Her family line would now continue! Further, by careful word choice, the author stressed something important about this child.

Normally, the Bible reports the sequence of marriage, conception, and birth like this: "So-and-so took such-and-such as his wife, and she conceived and bore a son." In this case, however, a key statement fell between the wife-taking and the childbearing. Literally, it says, "the Lord gave her conception." In other words, the newborn was more than just the product of human sexual activity. He was *a gift from God!*

In the Bible, that was a sign that the child would be someone special—a child of destiny. For example, remember the case of Sarah, Abraham's wife. After years of waiting, God enabled Sarah to bear a child (Gen. 21:1-2). His intervention was a sign that the child was the promised son of destiny. Likewise, God's intervention in Ruth's case marked that child as part of God's plan. Shortly, we will learn what that plan was. Bethlehem's good wishes would, indeed, turn out to be prophetic.

Now we see the first reason to celebrate God's goodness—because He rewards those who please Him. From the very beginning, the Book of Ruth hinted that God someday might reward Ruth. That was the gist of Naomi's prayer for Ruth and Orpah (Ruth 1:8) and Boaz's two prayers for Ruth (2:12; 3:10). As we saw, in paraphrase his words meant, "May the Lord give you a full paycheck for what you've done" (see chap. 6).

Here the Lord paid Ruth, not with dollars and cents, but with marriage and a newborn son. Her faithfulness had pleased God greatly. So He rewarded her greatly.

For forty years, Henry C. Morrison served as a missionary in Africa. Upon retirement, he boarded a ship back to America. As it happened, President Theodore Roosevelt was also on board. When the ship entered New York harbor, cheering thousands welcomed the President home. As Morrison watched the scene, he felt a little cheated.

He reviewed his forty years of service for Christ. He recalled the sacrifice, perseverance, suffering, and devotion required. "Surely, they deserve some sort of recognition," he thought. Suddenly, as he quietly pouted, Morrison heard a small voice. It said, "Henry—you're not home yet" (Michael P. Green, ed., *Illustrations for Biblical Preaching* [Grand Rapids: Baker, 1989], 306).

That is important for us to remember. Sometimes our present duties overwhelm us. Daily we juggle too many tasks—our family, our home, our job, and our church. Like Ruth and Henry Morrison, we labor to honor the Lord. But our payday never seems to come. We seem to reap nothing of what we have sown.

The life of Ruth reminds us that God *does* reward faithfulness, no matter how long it takes. Until that time, we are simply called to live lives pleasing to God. As we have learned, that is part of what faithfulness is.

The Celebration

Strikingly, the Bible quickly moved past Ruth and Boaz in Ruth 4:13. The story's climax starred Naomi and her new grandson, not Ruth and Boaz. That makes very good sense. The Book of Ruth is, in fact, more about Naomi than Ruth. It opened with her bitter suffering—exile, grief, and childlessness. The survival of her family line, not Ruth's, has hung in the balance. How appropriate, then, to feature Naomi at the book's end.

In the closing scene, Naomi and her friends celebrated the birth of her grandson. To begin, the neighbor women announced the birth to Naomi (v. 14). They said, "Praise be to the Lord, who this day has not left you without a kinsman-redeemer. May he become famous throughout Israel!" They called the newborn a "kinsman-redeemer" (i.e., a *gō'ēl*). This is the only application of the term to a child in the Old Testament. Then the women thanked God that the boy would take care of Naomi as she got older (see v. 15).

They also prayed that he would become a famous Israelite. Notice, however, that they did not give a simple news bulletin ("It's a boy!"). Instead, they broke the news in a brief psalm of praise to God. Full credit for this event, they said, belonged to the Lord. He was the story's real hero.

Now this is significant. Recall the roles played by God and the human characters in the book. God seemed to stay in the background most of the time. He acted directly only twice in the story. He gave Israel food after famine (1:6) and Ruth pregnancy after marriage (4:13).

Everything else happened because the human characters acted. On their own, Ruth gleaned, Naomi cooked up a plan, and Ruth carried it out. On his own, Boaz gave them food, went to court, and won the right to be redeemer. In the end, however, Naomi's neighbors gave all the credit to God. Why?

Long ago, someone wrote, "Sometimes providences, like Hebrew letters, must be read backward." That was the way Joseph "read" his life in Egypt. It had been no fun to be a slave and jailbird there. But, looking back, he saw that God had planned his bad experiences to bring good to Israel (Gen. 50:19-20). And the women "read" the story of Ruth and Naomi the same way.

Looking back, they calculated all the providences—the things which just happened to work out. Suddenly, it all made sense. They drew the obvious conclusion: God's guidance lay behind everything! No one had done anything on their own. The gentle, firm hand of God had guided every human step all along the way. This gives us a second reason to celebrate God's goodness—because He lovingly guides our lives.

Rev. John Klingberg experienced that guidance too. In 1903, he began to take in orphans in New Britain, Connecticut. Soon nearly two dozen of them shared a small rented home with his wife and two sons. The townspeople were supportive, but he only earned $16 a week as a pastor. That was hardly enough to support his large household. Like George Müeller in England, he trusted in God's timely provision.

One Sunday, however, the house finally ran out of food. Desperate, Pastor Klingberg knelt in prayer. In the background were sounds of people singing and having fun at the picnic ground up the street. Shutting out the noise, Klingberg closed his eyes and prayed, "The Lord is my Shepherd; I shall not want."

In mid-prayer, a torrential rain started to fall outside. Then, a knock at the door interrupted him. There stood two big, stocky fellows holding a huge hamper between them. "We're from the Bartenders' Union," one of them explained. "Rain broke up our picnic, and we thought you could use this stuff." In the hamper, Klingberg discovered huge hams, cheeses, sausages, bread and butter. "Thank you," said Klingberg, adding gently, "It is not entirely unexpected" (*The Bulletin* [of Fuller Theological Seminary], Winter 1988, p. 6).

Like the women, Klingberg knew that God lovingly directs our lives. God's timing is always perfect. At His direction, a rainstorm ruined a picnic just when Klingberg needed food. And our lives lie firmly in those same capable hands. With confidence, we can sing with the hymn writer:

He leadeth me, O blessed thought!
O words with heav'nly comfort fraught!
What-e'er I do, where-e're I be,
Still 'tis God's hand that leadeth me.

He leadeth me, He leadeth me,
By His own hand He leadeth me;

His faithful follower I would be,
For by His hand He leadeth me.

A Mother Again

At last, Naomi got to hold the precious child (Ruth 4:16). She took him from the women and laid him on her lap. In the Old Testament, that was the picture of the tender, motherly care given to infants (Num. 11:12; 1 Kings 3:20; Lam. 2:12). Some scholars believe that, by taking the child, Naomi performed a legal ritual, formally adopting him as her own son. In other words, the gesture was a legal symbol like that of handing over the sandal (see Ruth 4:7-8).

That seems unlikely, however. As another scholar noted, Naomi's act was one of love not law. The gesture looks more like a gentle mother's care than a legal proceeding. It is better understood as a touching human moment than as an official adoption.

At the same time, one should notice two important things about verse 16. First, a significant word from chapter 1—"child" (Heb. *yeled*)—has reappeared here. In verse 5, it referred to Naomi's lost sons, Mahlon and Kilion. By applying it to the newborn, the author probably wanted readers to remember the other sons. The word signaled that the "child" in Naomi's arms had replaced the two "children" who had died in Moab.

This completed another of the book's themes. Recall Naomi's bitter outburst that God had left her "empty" (Heb. *rêqām*)—that is, without husband or children (v. 21). Earlier, we noted that Boaz used the same word in giving Naomi grain (3:17; see chap. 10). The grain was a symbol that, if Ruth married, Naomi might get an heir and be "full" again. Thus, the newborn showed that God had restored Naomi to fullness.

Second, 4:16 says that Naomi "cared for him." Literally, the line read, "She became his foster mother." In the Old Testament, a foster mother (Heb. *'ōmenet*) was someone who took care of children whose parents could not (2 Sam. 4:4; 2 Kings 10:1, 5; Es. 2:7, 20). Obviously, Ruth was very much alive and capable of raising the baby. Why, then, would Naomi be its foster mother?

In many cultures, it is customary for parents to give grand-parents children to raise as their own children. In my view, that was the case here. If so, Ruth had given the child to Naomi as if he had been born to her. In other words, her "fullness" is not just symbolic but real. She had an actual son to raise.

That was why the women watching this scene shout, "Naomi has a son!" They used the traditional phrase with which Israelites announced the birth of a child (see Job 3:3; Isa. 9:6; Jer. 20:15). The neighbors had already announced the birth, however. So here the phrase served, not to announce, but to interpret the event.

It stressed that Naomi was no longer a widow without children. She had a son to carry on her line! Finally, the women named the boy Obed (lit. "servant"). The name meant that the boy would serve the Lord or Naomi (see Ruth 4:15) or both.

Now imagine how this scene contrasts the opening scene of Ruth 1. The negative has indeed produced a beautiful color print! (4:1) It is like the miracle of modern photography. Imagine the contrast between the original film and the finished picture. An ugly, colorless negative yields a beautiful color print. In Naomi's case, the negative (1:3, 5) has indeed produced a beautiful color print! (4:16)

Before, the women greeted Naomi as a ghost from the past: "Can this really be Naomi?" (1:19) Now they rejoiced over her motherhood: "Naomi has a son!" The empty woman Naomi now had a precious armful. The once bitter woman could not be more joyful. The barren widow now had a son. God had heard and answered her painful outcry. The seeds sown earlier had indeed born fruit!

My wife and I witnessed a similar scene. Some friends apparently could not have children. Ten years of marriage and many doctor visits had produced no results. Many times, we had listened with sympathy to their frustration and bitterness. They had simply given up. But God surprised them.

Celebration

Sometime later, they unexpectedly learned that the wife was pregnant. Tears of joy flowed freely the day we saw our friends holding their newborn son. With Naomi's neighbors, we joyously cried, "They have a son!" God had intervened for them too! This brings out the third reason for celebrating God's goodness—because God intervenes for those in need.

In ancient societies, widows, orphans, and aliens were especially defenseless. They lacked family to protect them from those wanting to take advantage of them. According to the Old Testament, however, God Himself was their protector. As Psalm 146:9 says, "The Lord watches over the alien and sustains the fatherless and the widow, but frustrates the ways of the wicked." He also watches over all His children in need. Whatever your need, He can meet it. God promises to intervene when His people need Him.

The Big Surprise!

The Book of Ruth was full of surprises. So, it is no surprise that it ended with another one. In Ruth 4:17, the author reported that the women gave Obed his name. Immediately, however, he added, almost as an afterthought, "He [Obed] was the father of Jesse, the father of David." In other words, the great King David was the great-grandson of Ruth and Boaz.

"OK, but so what?" you ask. To answer, let me use another example from modern photography—the zoom lens. This remarkable device enables a television camera to move easily between wide shots and close-ups. It can focus on the playing field, then slowly draw back to show the entire stadium.

I think the last line of verse 17 affects readers in a similar way. It quickly draws us back from a close-up of Naomi and Obed to show Israel's wider history. On screen, as it were, the two figures shrink to the left while another figure appears on screen to the right. The gleaming crown identifies the new figure as King David. The Bible writer wants us to make a connection between Ruth, Boaz, and David.

So what? The answer is this: were it not for Ruth and Boaz, there would have been no David. Their seeds of faithfulness produced him. God used them to give Israel its greatest leader. By making the connection, the writer added his commentary to the entire book.

In essence, he said, "How amazing! God multiplied Ruth's devotion, Naomi's cleverness, and Boaz's honesty! Their simple faithfulness gave Israel such greatness!" This tells us the final reason for celebrating God's goodness—because He multiplies our efforts to serve His purpose. As Paul put it, "[God] is able to do immeasurably more than all we ask or imagine, according to His power that is at work within us" (Eph. 3:20).

Edward Kimball was a Christian businessman living in Boston more than a hundred years ago. One day a teenager moved to town to work in his uncle's shoe store. He joined Kimball's Sunday School class, and Kimball often witnessed to him at the store. On April 21, 1855, the young man committed his life to Jesus Christ. Few people remember the layman, Edward Kimball.

Almost everyone, however, is familiar with the evangelist D.L. Moody. He was the teenager Kimball won to Christ. Thousands of people received Christ through Moody's preaching. Thousands more, graduates of Moody Bible Institute, have taken the Gospel around the world. Thousands more have received the Gospel through them (John C. Pollock, *Moody: A Biographical Portrait* [New York: Macmillan, 1963], 11–15).

Yet it all began with the simple faithfulness of an ordinary Christian, Edward Kimball. His life illustrates the main message of the Book of Ruth: God uses the faithfulness of ordinary people to do great things.

But back to my camera analogy again. Suppose we pull the camera lens back farther. Ruth, Boaz, and David get even smaller. Another royal figure, one much larger than David, appears at the right. This King is Jesus, a later Descendant of Ruth and Boaz (Matt. 1:5). He too is a product of their faithfulness.

Now imagine the lens retreating still farther. Soon you appear on screen with the others. Look around you carefully.

Celebration

Do you see the many people whose lives you touch every week? Some are your family, others the people you work with. There are neighbors or people with whom you regularly do business—the barber, beautician, baker, bank teller.

Finally, imagine the camera withdrawing as far as possible. At the right appears a joyous victory celebration. From His majestic throne, King Jesus surveys a crowd of millions, all His faithful followers. The crowd sings excitedly, their faces beaming with relief and joy.

Of course, you are there, but—surprise!—next to you are several people your life touched. They are there because you brought them the Gospel. Your seeds of simple faithfulness have also borne fruit!

"Me—of all people!" you say? On second thought, why not you? God used the simple faithfulness of Naomi, Ruth, and Boaz to do great things. Why should He not use yours? After all, His power can multiply your small efforts into many wonderful results.

Conclusion

Paul wrote to Christians at Corinth, "Whoever sows sparingly will also reap sparingly, and whoever sows generously will also reap generously" (2 Cor. 9:6). He was speaking of giving generous offerings to support poor Christians. The same principle, however, applies to our lives.

The more faithfully we live, the more we please God, the more seeds we sow. And the more seeds we sow, the greater our harvest. God calls us simply to live for Him wherever we are—at home, at work, in the neighborhood, and in church. If we do, His power will multiply our efforts for His glory.

In chapter 3, I wrote about the courage of Rosa Parks which sparked the boycott of city buses in Montgomery, Alabama. In December 1955, during that protest, Dr. Martin Luther King, Jr. spoke to the boycotters. His words still challenge Christians to live faithfully today:

Whatever your life's work is, do it well. A man should do his job so well that the living, the dead, and the unborn

155

could do it no better. If it falls your lot to be a street sweeper, sweep streets like Michelangelo painted pictures, like Shakespeare wrote poetry, like Beethoven composed music; sweep streets so well that all the host of Heaven and earth will have to pause and say, "Here lived a great street sweeper, who swept his job well."

Then Dr. King quoted poet Douglas Malloch:

> If you can't be a pine on the top of the hill
> Be a scrub in the valley—but be
> The best little scrub by the side of the hill.
> Be a bush if you can't be a tree."[8]

That is the faithfulness that God uses to do great things. Faithfulness means doing our best—whatever we are, wherever we are—for God's glory. Whatever our situation, God desires us to be faithful—and then to watch Him do great things through us.

Chapter Thirteen

Conclusion: The Lessons of Hindsight

Ruth 4:18-22

Every good story must have a good ending, resolving the story's tensions and conflicts. The hero rescues the afflicted and rides off happily into the sunset. The villain either reforms or goes to jail. That may be one reason the Book of Ruth is such a great story. It has three good endings!

In the first, Ruth and Boaz married, and Ruth had a son. That settled the book's primary problem—Naomi's need for an heir. In the second ending, the author announced that Naomi's newborn was King David's grandfather. He showed how the book's events later solved a desperate national crisis, a lack of leadership. Through Obed's grandson, David, God unified Israel and defeated her enemies.

The book's third ending, however, seems strange. The biblical author gave up storytelling and wrote a list of ancestors (Ruth 4:18-22). Now, at first glance, the list strikes us as dull reading. The phrase "X was the father of Y" drones on nine times in a row. The only breaks in the boredom are changes in the names of "X" and "Y." The temptation is to skip the verses and move on to something we consider more spiritual.

Actually, the author of Ruth included this list for a purpose. He felt it gave the book just the right closing touch. It looked at faithfulness from the perspective of hindsight. From that perspective, the Book of Ruth still has a few things to teach us.

The Genealogy: Its Background

Most of us are not into genealogies. We associate the word "genealogy" with old family Bibles and Mormons. We think of family Bibles because they often have pages for a family genealogy and of Mormons because of their famous archive of genealogies. But if we value genealogies only for entertainment, they have no practical use for us.

Other cultures, however, highly value them. Some African tribes take great pride in repeating a memorized genealogy of many generations. In the ancient world, ancestral lists served important practical ends. They helped determine whether or not certain near relatives could marry. They settled disputes over land ownership. They supported the claims of kings to thrones. They confirmed which priests were entitled to hold religious office.

To write this genealogy, the author of Ruth probably drew on palace records in Jerusalem. Most ancient kings had an official genealogy, and David was likely no exception. (Presumably, those records also shaped the genealogies in 1 Chron.) In fact, genealogies are the only record of five ancestors listed—Hezron, Ram, Amminadab, Salmon (or Salmah), and Obed.

This genealogy, however, has several striking features. First, like most biblical genealogies, the list is an incomplete one. Notice that it lists exactly ten generations. Evidently, the author tailored the list to fit that number by leaving out some ancestors. The time from Perez to David covered about 700 years (1700–1000 B.C.). Probably there are more than ten generations in that period. It is not likely that each ancestor fathered his son at age 70!

Apparently, the author also tailored the list to divide Israel's history into two major periods. The first five generations covered the period from Jacob to Moses—Perez, Hezron, Ram, Amminadab, and Nahshon (Ruth 4:18-20a). The final five covered the period from Moses to David—Salmon, Boaz, Obed, Jesse, and David (vv. 20b-22). That is, it listed five generations before the famous Exodus from Egypt and five after it.

Conclusion

Why did the genealogy have only ten members? The simplest answer is this: many genealogies of ancient kings had ten members. For example, some king-lists from ancient Sumer and Assyria have exactly ten names. So, the author of Ruth may have followed that format to show that this was a king's genealogy. Later, however, I will suggest that the format also contributed to the author's message.

Second, observe that the author followed another ancient genealogical practice. Ten-member genealogies reserved certain positions for people of special honor. Obviously, the most important position was the last one. In this case, David received this highest honor (v. 22). After all, it was his genealogy.

Interestingly, the position second in importance was the seventh one. In David's list, Boaz held it (v. 21). No one can quarrel with that. Boaz was one of the story's heroes. So, the genealogy followed up the book's love story. It gave Boaz an additional honor for rescuing Naomi's faltering family line. It gave him an honored place among David's famous ancestors.

The fifth position was the one of third importance. Significantly, its occupier was Nahshon, a remarkable leader from Israel's past. Nahshon was the brother-in-law of Aaron the priest, the brother of Moses. He was also chief of the tribe of Judah (Ex. 6:23; Num. 1:7; 2:3).

During Israel's stay at Mt. Sinai, Nahshon emerged as a key national leader. As a tribal chief, he assisted Moses in taking the first census. He was also the first tribal leader to present an offering at the tabernacle's dedication (Num. 7:12, 17). When Israel left Sinai, Nahshon led the way as the head of Judah, the leading tribe (10:14). Certainly, he was one of Israel's great early leaders.

Finally, the first position ranked fourth in importance. The list honored that ancestor as founder of the illustrious family line. In David's line, that honor went to Perez, one of twin sons born to Jacob's son Judah (Gen. 38). We noted earlier that Judah recognized the clan of Perez as one of its leading families (see chap. 11). So, the genealogy followed up the mention of Perez in the blessings of Ruth 4:12.

The Genealogy: Its Message

Why did this genealogy conclude the Book of Ruth? In my opinion, it helped to achieve the book's main purpose. Earlier, I mentioned that ancient genealogies supported the claims of kings to their thrones. In chapter 1, I also suggested that the book's purpose was to support David's claim to be king. The genealogy supported this claim by stressing three things.

First, it showed that David's family enjoyed God's special blessing. In the Bible, the survival and growth of a family line was a sign of God's grace. Recall how the Book of Genesis traced the line of Abraham for four generations. The line struggled to survive against famine, enemies, and infertility. It grew into twelve large tribal groups. That survival and growth testified to God's special blessing on Abraham's descendants.

The genealogy of David said the same thing about his family. It traced his line for ten generations. They survived and grew into a leading family group. God had, indeed, specially blessed them in a tangible way. They had the numbers to prove it!

Second, the genealogy stressed God's providential guidance of David's family line. Name by name, the genealogy spread out a sweeping panorama of providence. Here the number ten played a special role. In the Bible, it conveyed the idea of completeness and order.

That is another reason why the author of Ruth tailored the ancestral list to have ten members. That is also why he divided it into pre-Exodus and post-Exodus phases. The arrangement portrayed the development of David's family with a sense of order and completeness. In turn, that order implied that God's guiding hand stood behind it. Only God could have kept the line alive for so many generations. And only God could have orchestrated its rise to prominence in Israel.

Third, the genealogy stressed that David had the family credentials to rule Israel. Simply put, he had good breeding! David had descended from the great Nahshon, close associate of Moses and Aaron and famous Judean leader. He also descended from Perez, founder of one of Judah's leading families. So, David had the family background to serve as leader. He came from a clan to whom Israel had already looked for leadership.

In sum, the genealogy followed up the book's main story. It showed God's guidance and blessing in David's family. All this carried out the book's main purpose. It showed that God had specially given David to lead Israel.

The Genealogy: Its Lessons

Now you ask, "What can a dry genealogy teach me?" First, it reminds us of the value of spiritual hindsight. By "spiritual hindsight" I mean an occasional look back to see what God has done in our lives. Only then do we notice the fingerprints of His invisible work in us.

Sadly, most of us live under what someone called the "tyranny of the urgent." Life's urgent demands rule us like a terrible tyrant. Pressing present concerns always preoccupy us. We barely get done what must be done, much less anything more. There are always things to do, places to go, and people to see. Like cruel dictators, our watches and calendars control us.

Now it is a physical fact that the faster life goes, the less perspective one can get on it. For example, while stopped, a driver enjoys a full field of vision—180 degrees or more. At 60 m.p.h., however, the field of vision is barely wider than the beams of the car's headlights. The driver shuts out everything except what is just ahead.

But remember that hindsight is 20-20. As we look back, the larger landscape of our life emerges. In hindsight, we see clearly patterns and order we would otherwise miss. Only then can we realize how much we have grown spiritually. Only then can we recognize how much God has been doing in us. Only then do we learn what God has been doing through us.

My wife and I often get helpful hindsight during times away from home. A weekend in the mountains or a restful vacation provide us the right setting. We get the chance to observe our lives from a distance. Often, we return refreshed, praising God for the good things He is doing. Being so busy, we had not even noticed them!

Other times, we come back resolved to change some things. The changes may be bad attitudes or habits which hinder our growth. They may be opportunities for greater growth and service for God. Always, we see things we had not noticed before.

I encourage you to do the same thing, even if you cannot get away. Look back over the last few years. How has God changed you? How has God used you to touch the lives of others? Take a few moments to thank God for these things seen in spiritual hindsight. Also, what things in your life need changing? Ask God to guide you to embrace such changes.

Second, the genealogy reminds us that God's hand guides us. David's God is our God too. He sent David's greatest Son, Jesus, as our Savior. He drew us to personal faith in Christ. He still fully controls human history. We are still part of His larger plan—the salvation of the world. So we can rely on Him to guide our lives.

Too often the rush of daily life shuts out awareness of God's control. Our lives seem so chaotic. We have jobs to do, children to raise, and houses to maintain. We do our best to keep up with things, but there never seems to be enough time. Unplanned events—illnesses, accidents, natural disasters, and business failures—disrupt our lives.

Many times life makes no sense at all. Worse, it seems simply out of control. The genealogy, however, reminds us to stop and get a biblical picture of life. It calls us to look past the chaos and see God quietly working behind the scenes. It asks us to put our troubled hands into His strong hands once again.

That is what Marian Anderson always advised. Anderson was a black singer whose rich contralto voice delighted millions. The great conductor Toscanini once praised her voice as one "heard once in a hundred years." In 1939, racism denied her use of a concert hall in Washington, D.C. So she sang the concert at the Lincoln Memorial—and to 75,000 people!

Conclusion

For an encore, Anderson always observed a very special tradition. She always sang a song without orchestra or piano backup. And she always sang the same piece, the Negro spiritual "He's Got the Whole World in His Hands." The power of her voice left audiences silent, deeply moved. She sang from the depths of her own personal faith and experience. The song was her own personal testimony to the absolute sovereignty of God.

Your life may seem chaotic and out of control. You may wonder what tomorrow will bring—or even if there will be a tomorrow. The closing of the Book of Ruth, however, reminds us that someone *is* in charge. He holds our lives securely in His hands. Our lives are not out of control. With confidence, we can sing:

> He's got you and me, brother, in His hands,
> He's got you and me, sister, in His hands,
> He's got you and me, brother, in His hands,
> He's got the whole world in His hands.

The Challenge

As I said at the beginning, most Christians have a spiritual inferiority complex. They think that God only uses very specially gifted people. He only works through pastors, evangelists, and missionaries. And, of course, none of us qualify as specially gifted in God's sight. So, we sit on the sidelines of the kingdom while others enjoy His blessing.

But how wonderful that God put the Book of Ruth in our Bible! It reminds us that God uses all, not just some, of His people. He works through people who live faithfully for Him in daily life. All He wants from them is simple, down-to-earth faithfulness. He wants faithfulness in the way they do their jobs, love their families, help their neighbors, and serve their churches. He loves to see our faithfulness right on Main Street.

For years, Admiral Hyman Rickover headed the Navy's nuclear power program. He personally interviewed every officer who applied to serve in it. In his book *Why Not the Best?*

former President Jimmy Carter described his interview with Rickover.

For two hours, the unsmiling admiral grilled Carter on military and nonmilitary subjects. At first confident, Carter soon began to sweat. He realized how little he actually knew. Then, Rickover asked Carter how high he ranked in his class at the Naval Academy. Thinking he could redeem himself, Carter said proudly, "Sir, I stood 59th in a class of 820!"

Instead of congratulations, the admiral coldly asked, "Did you do your best?" Carter knew there was no sense bluffing Rickover with a hearty, "Yes, sir!" Sheepishly he replied, "No, sir, I didn't always do my best."

For a long moment, the admiral stared at Carter. Then he turned his chair around to end the interview. Finally, he asked one last, unforgettable question: "Why not?"[9]

That is the challenge which confronts all of us. Faced with this book's faithful ancestors, why not live faithfully ourselves? As the Book of Ruth teaches, when people are faithful, God uses them to do great things. By faithfulness in life's ordinary daily tasks, you sow the seeds of a great harvest for God's glory. Though just an ordinary Christian, God can use you! Why not?

Notes

1. Phyllis Trible, "A Human Comedy: The Book of Ruth," in *Literary Interpretations of Biblical Narratives,* Vol. II, ed. K. Gros Louis (Nashville: Abingdon, 1982), p. 173.

2. Charles W. Colson, *Born Again* (Old Tappan, N.J.: Chosen Books, 1976), p. 199.

3. D. Winton Thomas, ed., *Documents from Old Testament Times* (New York: Harper & Row, 1958), p. 201.

4. Corrie ten Boom, *The Hiding Place* (Washington Depot, Conn.: Chosen Books, 1971), p. 190.

5. James B. Pritchard, *Ancient Near Eastern Texts Relating to the Old Testament,* 3rd ed. (Princeton, N.J.: Princeton University Press, 1969), p. 639.

6. Beth Day, "The Little Professor of Piney Woods" found in the *Reader's Digest Con. Book,* vol. 68, May 1956, pp. 161–62.

7. Bezalel Porten, "The Scroll of Ruth: A Rhetorical Study," *Gratz College Annual* 7 (1978), p. 40.

8. Quoted from Stephen B. Oates, *Let the Trumpet Sound* (New York:

Mentor Books, 1982), p. 102.

9. Norman Polmar and Thomas B. Allen, *Rickover: Controversy and Genius* (New York: Simon and Shuster, 1982), p. 267.